Communications in Computer and Information Science 1727

Rationale

The CCIS series is devoted to the publication of proceedings of computer science conferences. Its aim is to efficiently disseminate original research results in informatics in printed and electronic form. While the focus is on publication of peer-reviewed full papers presenting mature work, inclusion of reviewed short papers reporting on work in progress is welcome, too. Besides globally relevant meetings with internationally representative program committees guaranteeing a strict peer-reviewing and paper selection process, conferences run by societies or of high regional or national relevance are also considered for publication.

Topics

The topical scope of CCIS spans the entire spectrum of informatics ranging from foundational topics in the theory of computing to information and communications science and technology and a broad variety of interdisciplinary application fields.

Information for Volume Editors and Authors

Publication in CCIS is free of charge. No royalties are paid, however, we offer registered conference participants temporary free access to the online version of the conference proceedings on SpringerLink (http://link.springer.com) by means of an http referrer from the conference website and/or a number of complimentary printed copies, as specified in the official acceptance email of the event.

CCIS proceedings can be published in time for distribution at conferences or as post-proceedings, and delivered in the form of printed books and/or electronically as USBs and/or e-content licenses for accessing proceedings at SpringerLink. Furthermore, CCIS proceedings are included in the CCIS electronic book series hosted in the SpringerLink digital library at http://link.springer.com/bookseries/7899. Conferences publishing in CCIS are allowed to use Online Conference Service (OCS) for managing the whole proceedings lifecycle (from submission and reviewing to preparing for publication) free of charge.

Publication process

The language of publication is exclusively English. Authors publishing in CCIS have to sign the Springer CCIS copyright transfer form, however, they are free to use their material published in CCIS for substantially changed, more elaborate subsequent publications elsewhere. For the preparation of the camera-ready papers/files, authors have to strictly adhere to the Springer CCIS Authors' Instructions and are strongly encouraged to use the CCIS LaTeX style files or templates.

Abstracting/Indexing

CCIS is abstracted/indexed in DBLP, Google Scholar, EI-Compendex, Mathematical Reviews, SCImago, Scopus. CCIS volumes are also submitted for the inclusion in ISI Proceedings.

How to start

To start the evaluation of your proposal for inclusion in the CCIS series, please send an e-mail to ccis@springer.com.

Revathi Venkataraman · Annie Uthra ·
Vijayan Sugumaran · R. I. Minu ·
Pethuru Raj Chelliah
Editors

Internet of Things

Third International Conference, ICIoT 2022
Chennai, India, April 5–7, 2022
Revised Selected Papers

 Springer

Editors
Revathi Venkataraman (iD)
SRM Institute of Science and Technology
Kattankulathur, India

Annie Uthra (iD)
SRM Institute of Science and Technology
Kattankulathur, India

Vijayan Sugumaran (iD)
Oakland University
Rochester, MI, USA

R. I. Minu (iD)
SRM Institute of Science and Technology
Kattankulathur, India

Pethuru Raj Chelliah (iD)
Reliance Jio Platforms Ltd.
Bangalore, India

ISSN 1865-0929   ISSN 1865-0937 (electronic)
Communications in Computer and Information Science
ISBN 978-3-031-28474-8   ISBN 978-3-031-28475-5 (eBook)
https://doi.org/10.1007/978-3-031-28475-5

This Springer imprint is published by the registered company Springer Nature Switzerland AG
The registered company address is: Gewerbestrasse 11, 6330 Cham, Switzerland

Preface

This volume contains the refereed and selected papers presented at the 3rd edition of the International Conference on Internet of Things (ICIoT 2022) from April 5th to 7th, 2022 in the School of Computing, SRM Institute of Science and Technology, Kattankulathur, India.

The conference aimed to provide an outstanding opportunity for both academic and industrial communities to address new trends and challenges in emerging technologies and progress in standards on topics relevant to today's fast-moving technology trends in the Internet of Things. It also provided a platform for the discussion of new results in the field of the Internet of Things. Different themes were addressed on each day and each theme contained different thought-provoking sessions. The first-day sessions focused on the application of IoT in the field of Computer Science and Information Technology. On the second day, start-ups and entrepreneurs shared their success stories and experiences in implementing IoT, and a few sessions focused on Industrial IoT.

Government initiatives like Digital India, Smart Cities, where top bureaucrats from various departments will deliberate on the themes during the last day of the Conference. Researchers, faculty, students, and practitioners presented their findings and ideas during the paper presentation session on all three days. The conference was inaugurated on 5th April 2022 with dignitaries from SRM IST, Australia, USA, Canada, Singapore, and Ireland.

In response to the call for papers, ICIoT 2022 received 212 submissions from authors from countries including Australia, Turkey, Lithuania, and Saudi Arabia.

Out of 100 submissions, the Program Committee (PC) recommended only 53 papers for conference presentation, out of which 10 papers are included in this volume. Each submission was reviewed by at least three PC members or invited reviewers, experts in their fields, in order to supply detailed and helpful comments.

The conference featured ten invited lectures:

- Chandaram Sivaji, DST, India "Recent Research Opportunities"
- Wei Xiang, La Trobe University, Australia "Integration of AI and Machine Learning"
- San Murugesan, Western Sydney University, Australia "Leveraging IOT to Create a Sustainable Environment"
- Aparna Kasinath, Syngene International, Ltd., India "Pharma and IOT: how these two dissolve filling connection?"
- Srini Sampalli, Dalhousie University, Canada "How IoT Can Shape the Future of Healthcare: Potential and Challenges"
- Vijayan Sugumaran, Oakland University, USA "Integrating Mixed Reality and Artificial Intelligence into Building Information Modeling: A Collaborative Tunnel Emergency Drill Management System"
- Atreyi Kankanhalli, National University of Singapore, Singapore "Pervasive Healthcare, Wearables, Gamification and Personalization"

- Raj Gururaj, University of Southern Queensland, Australia "Opportunities in IoT and its Alignment with Curriculum: Drivers, Barriers, Dilemmas and Solutions"
- Susan Xujuan Zhou, University of Southern Queensland, Australia "Early Detection of Chronic Health Conditions Using AI Prediction Models"
- Ranga Rao Venkatesha Prasad, Delft University of Technology, Netherlands "Extreme IOT"

We thank the authors for their submissions, and the members of the PC and external reviewers for their efforts in providing exhaustive reviews.

April 2022

Revathi Venkataraman
Annie Uthra
Vijayan Sugumaran
R. I. Minu
Pethuru Raj

Organization

Program Chair

Revathi Venkataraman   SRMIST, India

Program Committee Chairs

B. Amutha   SRMIST, India
M. Pushpalatha   SRMIST, India
R. Annie Uthra   SRMIST, India
P. Annapoorani   SRMIST, India
M. Lakshmi   SRMIST, India

Advisory Board

Raj Gururajan   University of Southern Queensland, Australia
Raghavendra B. Jana   Center for Computational and Data-Intensive
       Science and Engineering (CDISE), India
Sudha Jam   Stanford University, USA
Abdel-Hamid Mourad   United Arab Emirates University, UAE
Arijit Ray Chowdhury   Georgia Institute of Technology, USA
Bhaskar Krishnamachari   University of Southern California, USA
Lim Chwee Teck   National University of Singapore, Singapore
Maode Ma   Nanyang Technological University, Singapore
P. S. Neelakanta   Florida Atlantic University, USA
Rahul Jain   National University of Singapore, Singapore
Subhas Mukhopadhyay   Massey University, New Zealand
Takuro Sato   Waseda University, Japan
Tulika Mitra   National University of Singapore, Singapore
Kavitha Kumarappan   DXC Technology Asia, Singapore
Shuai Li   Swansea University, UK
Stephen Olatunde Olabiyisi   Ladoke Akintola University of Technology,
       Nigeria
Ali Kashif Bashir   Manchester Metropolitan University, UK
Basim Alhadidi   Al-Balqa' Applied University, Jordan
Eike Schallehn   Otto-von-Guericke-Universitaet, Germany

Eleni Mangina	University College Dublin (UCD), Ireland
Jenn-Wei Lin	Fu Jen Catholic University, Taiwan
Luca Pappalardo	University of Pisa, Italy
Meenalosini Vimal Cruz	Keene State College, USA
Shamala Subramaniam	Universiti Putra Malaysia, Malaysia
Anurag Kumar	Indian Institute of Science, India
C. E. Veni Madhavan	Indian Institute of Science, India
Kumar Padmanabh	Robert Bosch Corporate Research, India
P. Vijay Kumar	Indian Institute of Science, India
Sudeshna Sarkar	IIT Kharagpur, India
Anandakumar	Anna University, India
Baskar	Anna University, India
H. Khanna Nehemiah	Anna University, India
A. Kannan	Indian Institute of Technology, India
D. Devaraj	Kalasalingam University, India
R. Golda Brunei	Govt. College of Engineering, India
Nepoleon	SRM IST, India

Technical /Review Members

Vijayan Sugumaran	Oakland University, USA
C. Pethuru Raj	Reliance Jio Platforms Ltd., India
Gang Li	Deakin University, Australia
Sami Mahmoud Ouali	University of Technology and Applied Sciences, Ibri, Sultanate of Oman
Ganesan	Oakland University, USA
Priyadarsi Nanda	University of Technology Sydney (UTS), Australia
Maheswaran Gopalakrishnan	KTH Royal Institute of Technology, Sweden
Julien Cordry	Teesside University, UK
S. Hyder Ali	Burayadah Colleges, Saudi Arabia
T. S. Arulnanath	MLR Institute of Technology, India
Sandra Johnson	R.M.K. Engineering College, India
P. Chitra	Thyagaraja College of Engineering, India
P. Chitra	Meenakshi Sundararajan Engineering College, India
J. Shanthini	Dr. N. G. P. Institute of Technology, India
B. Prathusha Lakshmi	RMK College of Engineering and Technology, India
R. Thiagarajan	Prathyusha Engineering College, India
Balamurugan P.	Vellore Institute of Technology, India

T. Rajendran	Saveetha School of Engineering, India
C. Karthikeyan	KL University, India
Anatharaman G. R.	Mala Reddy Institute of Engineering and Technology, India
R. Jothikumar	Shadan College of Engineering & Technology, India
J. Amudhavel	Vellore Institute of Technology, India
T. Sudhakar	Vellore Institute of Technology, India
Murugan R.	Jain University, India
Dileep A. D.	Indian Institute of Technology Mandi, India
Veningston K.	National Institute of Technology Srinagar, India
Sitara K.	National Institute of Technology (NIT), India
Ghanshyam S. Bopche	National Institute of Technology (NIT), India
M. Venkatesan	NITK, India
Devasena G.	IIIT, India
N. Sivakumar	Pondicherry Engineering College, India
Sivabalakrishnan M.	Vellore Institute of Technology, India
S. Thanga Ramya	RMD Engineering College, India

Organizers

S. S. Sridhar	SRMIST, India
E. Poovammal	SRMIST, India
B. Amutha	SRMIST, India
G. Vadivu	SRMIST, India
Lakshmi C.	SRMIST, India
C. Malathy	SRMIST, India
D. Malathi	SRMIST, India
A. Jeyasekar	SRMIST, India
G. Niranjana	SRMIST, India
M. Murali	SRMIST, India
R. I. Minu	SRMIST, India
K. Vijaya	SRMIST, India
G. Maragatham	SRMIST, India

Contents

Enhanced RPL to Control Congestion in IoT: A Review

Aastha Maheshwari[1]([✉]), Rajesh K. Yadav[1], and Prem Nath[2]

[1] Computer Science and Engineering Department, Delhi Technological University,
Delhi, India
aasthamaheshwari.am@gmail.com, rkyadav@dtu.ac.in
[2] Computer Science and Engineering Department, H N B Garhwal University,
Srinagar, Uttarakhand, India

Abstract. In recent years, Internet of things (IoT) has been used and contributed in various applications by connecting various devices to each other through the internet. IoT is considered an interesting and emerging area that is used in various applications like smart environment, healthcare, smart city, and others. To make life simpler various low-power devices and sensors have been used which provide various services. IoT networks are majorly composed of low power devices and weakly connected devices as communication is through wireless medium where the interference of noise and link breakdown is high. Hence, routing protocol is for low power and lossy network (RPL) is needed. RPL is the routing protocol that is used to transmit data in an IoT network. RPL is developed by the internet engineering task force for routing in low power and lossy network. It is the only protocol which is standardized for routing in IoT network. Although RPL still faces various problems like stability, mobility, congestion issue as initially RPL is not designed by considered the IoT network requirements. In this paper congestion issue is focused and discussed several past solutions given by various authors to enhance the RPL protocol and tried to control congestion in the IoT network. The paper surveyed various literature works that define different metrics to control congestion or define different ways of routing by manipulating the standards of RPL. In this survey, papers are thoroughly studied, analyze the benefits and limitations of the approaches and also mention the future scope of the problem.

Keywords: Routing Protocol for Low Power and Lossy Network (RPL) · Congestion Control · Internet of Things (IoT)

1 Introduction

The Internet of Things (IoT) is the interconnection and integration of devices, embedded with computational power. It is a rapidly growing notion in the recent era. This concept is not theoretical anymore; it has been becoming an imperative part of our daily lives. With numerous use cases, from smart homes to automated

R. Venkataraman et al. (Eds.): ICIoT 2022, CCIS 1727, pp. 1–13, 2023.
https://doi.org/10.1007/978-3-031-28475-5_1

driving structures, IoT is advancing a great deal. The expected number of IoT devices in existence by 2025 is around 75.44 billion.

This demonstrates a five-fold escalation of the number over a decade [1]. These devices are increasingly being used in connected work and city applications in the past years, with household operations constituting about fifty percent of the connections between these devices [2]. Low-Power and Lossy Networks (LLNs) are the type of network, where the networks of IoT devices should take into account a variety of restrictions like storage space, computational power, and used energy since a vast number of these devices have scarce resources [3].

A great part of IoT systems comprises of LLNs, and so crafting improvements to their drawbacks hold outstanding value to academia and industry. In this regard, enhancing stability and diminishing the energy consumed by LLNs, is the prime focus of research lately [4]. Routing Protocol for Low-Power and Lossy Networks (RPL) is a recognized routing protocol for providing bidirectional connectivity for resourceconstrained device networks [5].

Multipoint-to-point (MP2P) communication is primarily supported by RPL. However, it also supports point-to-point (P2P) and point-to-multipoint (P2MP) network traffic. Research claims great potential for RPL to improve but few drawbacks should be acknowledged. These draw-backs include neglecting stability, a tendency towards load imbalance, congestion-free routing, and mobility is not considered well. Due to these shortcomings, RPL could not be accepted as a routing standard which is crucial now as the projection for the number of IoT devices is increasing significantly in the coming 10 years [6]. Works which focus on the handling of congestion issue by performing load balancing and routing in a congestion-free manner are examined in this survey. This survey is done by performing an extensive search on Google Scholar. Congestion issue is discussed by few authors and only survey [7,8] discussed it; however, unlike this study, they have not thoroughly targeted this topic.

The rest of the paper are as follows: In Sect. 2, general information of RPL is explained. Section 3 elaborates the previous work on RPL based congestion control with its benefits and drawbacks. In Sect. 4, the conclusion and the future scope are discussed.

2   Routing Protocol for Low Power and Lossy Network (RPL)

For RPL, the ROLL group published an RFC, as tasked by the IETF in the year 2012 [9]. The further RFCs have been published since then, which elaborate the prime workings of RPL, known as objective function [10,11], routing metrics. [12] and Trickle timer [13], In this section, the basic concept of RPL is explained.

RPL procures multi-hop paths from a leaf node to a root node through multiple intermediate nodes. Here, a destination-oriented Directed Acyclic Graph (DAG) called DODAG, is formed that maneuvers multi-point to-point traffic. Set of Potential node is selected by each node, for the next-hop selection on path towards the root. Since DAG allows a node to have several nodes as parents, it is beneficial over a tree by being more critical of link failures. A scalar quantity representing the cost of a link/node is called the Rank. The application-dependent OF determines the computation of Rank. The rank is used to determine nodes relative position in the DODAG which further aids in avoiding the formation of a loop.

The parent node rank is al-ways smaller than its child node where 16-bit monotonic scalar is used for rank. The DODAG helps to determine the preferred parent of the node among various other possible options. Thus, the preferred parent node is got selected when a node wants to transfer a packet to the root node, it directs the packet to the parent node which is preferred in the graph. This process will be continued as the selected parent node will further send the packet to its parent until the packet is received by the root node. DODAG is populated with the data related to the parent by the RPL protocol. To transfer the DODAG information, control packets are used named DIO (DODAG Information Object) and DIS (DODAG Information Solicitation). Various routing metrics like path and node and OF modulates the shaping of the DODAG. The process of formation of DODAG is elucidated in the listed steps.

- Firstly, the root of DODAG is determined which in turn initiates the transfer of DIO messages by performing local multicast. In case a node requests to the root node for DIO, the DIO is sent at once by the DODAG root. The rank of the DIO sender is present in these messages.
- The root sends the DIO to its neighboring nodes and they will process it in the same condition from a lower rank node. Then, the root node will be selected as their parent. Then further link-local multicast DIOs message is transferred by these nodes to other nodes. The rank is calculated of the node after receiving the DIOs by considering the OF and rank of the DIO sender. This step updates the message's rank field and the DIO is forwarded to other nodes.
- From the neighboring nodes which had sent DIO to these nodes, each node forms a parent set. Based on OF, a preferred parent is determined for the upcoming hops in upstream routes from the set of parents formed. Using DIO messages, DODAG is sustained after its formation.

It performs Routing Downward. Unlike the name 'downward' suggests, the messages are sent in the upwards direction towards the root. RPL uses a different signaling packet called DAO messages to transmit destination data upwards along with the graph in order to set up downward routes. Concerning control messages flow, RPL acts as a hierarchical network. Only after the creation of DODAG or topology via DIOs control messages transmission and exchange, the DAOs are transmitted. There are two modes for managing and storing downward routes in RPL.

3   Related Work on Congestion Handling in RPL

It has been observed that congestion is one of the major issues that occur in multihop routing, due to the increase of accumulated data as an increase in the count of hops. This causes node-level congestion. The risk of congestion is higher as a large number of devices transmitting the data at a higher rate and cause both node level and channel level congestion [8,14]. Due to the problem of congestion the reliability of the network gets impacted. Congestion causes unnecessary delays, packet loss, and high energy consumption [15]. Congestion is handled by performing traffic flow control, rerouting the traffic, or effectively balancing the load.

In [16], authors proposed an approach to handle the issue of congestion by using the concept of duty cycle. This controls the 6LoWPAN network traffic (DCCC6). The traffic is adjusted based on the occupancy of buffer and RDC. The routing part is handled by RPL. They deployed the 25 nodes randomly for testing the performance. They show both practical and simulation results and the performance is increase in terms of energy consumption and delay. In [17], authors proposed deaf, griping, and fuse as a congestion control scheme. They use buffer length and queue length to control the congestion. The combination of both is used in the approach fuse, which combines the length of both buffer and queue. This outperforms as compare to griping and deaf.

In [18], authors proposed the theoretical approach for congestion control by considering the priority of a node or an application. The framework uses the game theory concept and able to estimate the adaptive transmission rate for sensor nodes. Buffer, energy, and priority are considered while creating the game formula. The performance is increased in terms of delay, energy consumption, and throughput as shown in simulation results. In [19], authors proposed the approach based on resource control. The least congested path is detected based on the buffer occupancy. The approach is suitable for RPL/COAP based networks. It performs well in case of the congested network however doesn't work well for a non- congested network. The approach consumes high energy as packets are passively listened to by nodes when it is received as "eavesdropping" is used by the algorithm. An author in [20] performs load balancing to handle congestion. In this approach, node sends the congestion information to its child node based on the queue occupancy. DIO message is utilized to notify the child node. This approach improves the network performance when the network is congested.

The game theory-based approach is designed to select the new parent node if the node gets congested [21,22]. The information is sent by parent node to child node so that parent node can be changed by them. So, the communication will be reliable. The approach is compared by native RPL and results improvement of 100% throughput. The other way of load balancing by selecting multiple parent nodes which is opt by [23,24]. In this approach, load distribution is done by selecting different routes to transmit data. The approach is beneficial to avoid congestion and to improve throughput and energy efficiency. The approach changes the process of DODAG formation and the RPL standards get modified which causes the compatibility issue with native RPL. In [25] multipath routing is adopted to control the congestion problem in the network. The data is delivered by using multipath, the selection is done based on the objective function. When the congestion occurs, DOI message is used to notify and initiate the multipath operation. The concept of the grey theory is used in [26] to control the congestion by considering multiple parameters and perform an optimization approach by considering occupancy of buffer, delay, and Expected Transmission count. In this approach, both traffic and resource control are combined and uses utility functions to increase the throughput. In [27], authors proposed a method that witnesses reduction of consumed energy, this is achieved by using probability measure in traffic forwarding to the destined parents which balanced the load better. The administration of broadcast is at whole monitored by a new measure being introduced as Expected Lifetime (ELT). This measure identifies the nodes in our system which could be potential bottlenecks. When the algorithm moves into a phase of selection of parent, the described lifetime measure contribute as a pivotal factor in which parents possessing topmost values of ELT will ultimately obtain a rank lower compared to for whom we are finding the parent itself and hence lifetime consideration of potential bottlenecks is taken cared for. Thus, we obtain a topology that is balanced and has numerous parents and each parent is sharing the load of their children. Finally, the parent's ELT values and regressing traffic weight is decided parent selection. The results shows the lifetime of network getting better and load being more balanced throughout the network. Still, potential fragmentation may occur and the algorithm demands enhancement to tackle it. The extension is given in [28], which tackles the convergence of network and potential instabilities more smoothly.

In [25], the issue of congestion in the network is handled in M-RPL (Multipath RPL) which is an extension of RPL making use of a two-pronged approach. The first prong is congestion detection which utilizes PDR measures to deduce if a path possesses congestion. In case of congestion is there, then the second prong is of congestion avoidance in which the rate of forwarding to the node which is congested is diminished and alternative paths are made use of in routing the traffic. Though extra processing overhead of two executing the two prongs exist but the approach of MRPL has bolstered the overall throughput with congestion being reduced significantly when compared with standard RPL.

The objective function enhancement of RPL has been proposed in [28], named as LB-OF, which resolves the issue of balancing the load of the network when nodes that are bottlenecks are involved. The children of node which is the bottleneck is dispersed in surroundings to other parents having the same nodes as children making use of a new measure named as CNC (child node count). With the CNC measure, a node possessing a lower rank has made acceptance of new children a high priority whereas higher rank nodes would be reluctant to new children acceptance. The results showcase the lifetime of network being improved and the load on nodes getting balanced effectively, though power consumed in the network rises and nodes experiencing a frequent change in parents may administer instability in the network.

In [29], the approach utilizes smart grids for improvement of RPL which spreads out load and leads to better balancing of the network load and is called Objective Function for Quality of Service. The proposal brings out a measure called OFQS that takes into account latency, quality of the link, and residual energy. The approach has been derived from MRHOF which has retained the process used for calculation rank of nodes but has established thresholds to stabilize the routes by dealing with issue of parent changes for nodes happening quite frequently. The benefit of balancing of load achieved has enabled traffic to take routes that are less reliable and are longer. Also, network lifetime has improved. Notable point is that experiment was performed with count of nodes being kept low, but the experiment saw an extension with increased count of nodes in [30].

The authors in [23], taking the inspiration from behavior of flowing water, a new scheme Multi-gateway Load Balancing Scheme for Equilibrium (MLEq) was proposed which handles balancing of the load in distributed and dynamic manner. The networks possessing multiple DODAGs make use of this approach by implementing a rank parameter similar to the oneused in DODAG, called a virtual level (VL) metric. The approach tries to reduce congestion caused by the traffic of messages. If the VL value is high then it gives a signal that message traffic is high and thus we should begin shifting the junction of DODAGs which are overloaded to areas where the message traffic is less. Special messages called VIO (VL Information Object) are utilized to transmit VL metric as a multicast to every neighbor. The VIO message received with the hop distance being the shortest is selected to calculate the node's VL. The DODAGs' VL metric value determines the final topology of nodes to get the desired balancing of load. The downside of scheme is that energy consumed is higher than standard RPL due to the routing of special VIO messages.

In [31], authors propose the extension to RPL, named Heuristic Load Distribution Algorithm, which is a braided [32] multipath enhancement. It administers combination of two mechanisms: The first one is multipath routing which makes the nodes possess more than one parent simultaneously. The second one is Tangential Load Balancing used for balancing energy consumed in the network. Combination of both results in significant improvement in throughput, enhanced lifetime, and smoother balancing of load in network, though it may not showcase such improvements in case of situations in real life where the topology of network can be heterogeneous.

In [33], another method for multipath routing is proposed called Load-Balanced Data Collection through Opportunistic Routing (ORPL-LB) which employs a different mechanism than that of traditional mechanisms when the next hop is being selected. As opposed to pre- determination of route from which packet will travel, in ORPL-LB, there is a dynamic selection of next hop for the packet based on which next node is available in route, thereby avoiding congestion in paths. The Opportunistic routing when considers the responsibility of balancing of load becomes ORPL-LB which implements an interesting idea of sleep/wake-up to select the node which becomes packet's next hop. The nodes in sleep state are the ones dealing with traffic being high or energy being low and are thus avoided as potential candidates for the packet's next hop. The results are promising with reduction in duty cycles of nodes and having no negative impact on either success of packet delivery or delay in packet delivery.

With the need for the parent selection process to be dynamic, the authors in [34], introduce "Energy-Aware and Load Balanced Parent Selection" which aims to reduce energy consumed and load being balanced effectively amongst nodes. The IEEE 802.15.4 [8], standard's topology, the cluster- tree MAC is modified which aims at distribution of traffic more uniformly. This modification is RPL compatible as well as allows selection of more than one parent. Every node transmits the packet to parent node which is selected based on combination of two factors. The first one is the residual energy of the parent node and the second is how much load in the parent path has experienced recently. This cluster-tree MAC approach is novel method extending the lifetime of network, providing reduction in end- to-end delays and improving ratio of successful packet delivery which ultimately enhances the overall performance of network.

Authors in [35], showcase an approach called Minimum Degree RPL which uses spanning trees of minimum degree to incorporate RPL with better load balancing. With the use of such spanning trees of minimum degree, the resultant network would be broader instead of being taller and network congestion will reduce. The approach has four stages. First, the determination of the tree's highest degree node takes place. The second stage sees those nodes possessing the highest degree look for an alternate edge to a node possessing a lower degree. The third stage is used if multiple alternative edges are recognized for a node and thus is an optional stage. The final stage is responsible for swapping the nodes to finally reduce the degree of the node possessing the highest degree. It leads to good results with 15.6% reduced consumption of energy in the network which increases network lifetime.

In [36], authors proposed the method called Load Balanced Routing for RPL (LBRPL), which solves the problem of imbalanced load with reliability and in a decentralized way. The model is created analytically in which limited resources of the node are quantified. It is established that count of nodes that have actually been sending the packets server as an important factor for the delivery rate or successful delivery ratio of the packet. The model follows an approach having dual goals. The determination of how much imbalance of load exists in- network is the first goal. For this, monitoring of buffer utilization is done by seeing how much buffer is filled up during time different intervals. If load is high on buffers, DIO message transmission can be deferred to reduce congestion and workload. The second goal is to forward data in a loadbalanced way in which suitable less congested parent is identified to which the packet should be forwarded. The model helps to reap benefits of reduced loss of packets, lower latencies and uniform spread of workload in network.

In [37], authors proposed an approach based on AI and machine learning called LBO-QL (Load Balanced Optimization based on Q Learning) makes use of Q Learning which checks the count of children for a parent node for balance in network. Each node just keeps information of immediate parents to reduce overheads. The approach experiences quicker convergence and lesser control messages in contrast to standard RPL. The drawback is its limited scalability due to the dependence of Q Learning algorithm on the network hub for purposes of calculations.

In [38], a new protocol based on fuzzy logic called Fuzzy Logic-based EnergyAware (FLEA) RPL is used for better distribution of energy and load on nodes. While fuzzy logic is utilized for several enhancement proposals to RPL [39, 40], but an approach that takes care of balancing the load as well is something novel. FLEA-RPL involves setting up one linguistic variable each for three metrics selected for routing which are ETX, Load, and Residual Energy. A "Quality" measure is calculated based on fuzzification rules and this quality measure is employed in the selection of the parent node. The results reveal an improved lifetime of the network and more success in packet delivery. The residual energy of nodes is uniformly distributed and has led to better balancing of the overall load in the network. The present short comings of the method are no support for mobility and stability of network has reduced.

In [41], congestion is controlled by performing offloading the data packets to the neighbor nodes to reduce the congestion of the overloaded node. The neighbor node is selected by using the mathematical model to predict the congestion level of in range nodes. In [42], congestion prediction is focused by applying the machine learning model to predict the congested node in the network. This model results high accuracy prediction but the energy consumption is high due to the machine learning model.

In [26], the problem of congestion is focused for 6LowPAN network where congestion is handled by performing resources control or traffic control approach. The authors proposed a hybrid approach where parent node is selected based on the congestion condition which is analyzed by buffer occupancy, ETX and delay. The node congestion value is calculated by applying grey relational analysis. It also controls the transmission rate by calculating it by using Lagrange multipliers and KTT conditions. The approach worked better for throughput, network lifetime, packet loss and delay as compare to QU-RPL and DCCC6. The approach is not considering the impact of neighbor and the mobility in the network.

In [43], authors proposed a fuzzy logic-based parent node selection approach for congestion avoidance. They focused on the optimal route selection for data transmission. Authors considered route status, transmission count, and buffer occupancy for the selection of the parent node. For the multiple parameters, decision-making approaches used a fuzzy weighted sum model. The model dynamically switches the route by checking the status of congestion and select the non-congested route. This approach performs better as compared to QU-RPL and OHCA. It increases network throughput and reduces packet loss. However, the authors didn't consider the mobility in the network which is common in real-time IoT networks.

It has been observed the load-balancing is one of the major ways to avoid congestion in the network. Multipath routing is also performed to distribute the data through multiple paths or to keep the alternative path to handle the situation of congestion. The new parent node selection process is another important aspect used by the child node when old parent node gets congested, so depends on various parameters new parent node gets selected based on its congestion state. The performance of all the surveyed approach for the congestion control is examined based on the network throughput, packet loss rate, latency and the network lifetime (Table 1).

Table 1. Comparison table of recent work

Ref No	Parameter/Concept used	Benefits	Limitations
[16]	Concept of Duty cycle is used. Control traffic transmission	Reduce delay, improve energy efficiency	- Does not support mobility - Reduce throughput - Does not use uncongested Node
[17]	Buffer occupancy	Improve energy efficiency and packet delivery ratio	- Does not support mobility - Reduce throughput - Does not use uncongested Node
[18]	Adaptive transmission rate	Reduce delay, improve packet delivery ratio and throughput support priority of packet	- Does not support mobility - Does not use uncongested Node
[19]	Bird flocking technique	Improve packet delivery ratio	- Does not support mobility - Consume more energy
[20]	Queue occupancy	Improve energy efficiency and packet delivery ratio Better load balancing	- Does not support mobility - Does not use uncongested Node
[21] [22]	Queue occupancy Game theory to find non congested path	Improve throughput and packet delivery ratio	- Does not support mobility - Increase energy consumption
[23] [44] [45]	Find multiple parent node	Improve throughput and energy	- Does not support mobility - Does not support RPL standards
[24]	Multipath routing	Improve throughput and energy efficiency perform better load balancing	- Does not support mobility
[25] [26]	Adaptive Multipath routing	Enhance Throughput, delay and energy efficiency. Perform load balancing	- Does not support mobility - Does not support and Increase computation overhead
[25]	ETX Residual Energy Traffic control	Reduce Energy consumption	- Fragmentation causes high risk
[28]	Packet delivery ratio	Increased Throughput	- Considered lower number of Nodes High overhead
[29]	Multipath Routing Rate of transmission controlled	Increase network lifetime	- Comparison to other method is less

(*continued*)

Table 1. (*continued*)

Ref no	Parameter/concept used	Benefits	Limitations
[30] [23]	ETX, Delay and Residual Energy	Increased network lifetime and packet delivery ratio	- Reduce stability, Frequent change in parent node
[31]	Multipath routing	Increase network capacity	- Increase energy consumption
[32]	Hop count and route cost	Increase throughput	- No real testbed
[33]	Opportunistic routing	Reduce Duty cycle without causing Delay	- Comparison to other method is less
[34]	Residual energy Node load	packet Increased delivery ratio and network lifetime	- Increase overhead
[35]	Minimum spanning tree is used to adjust the load of overloaded node	Reduce power consumption	- High message overhead Evaluated with a low number of nodes
[36]	DIO message is used to transmit congested node	Better network workload spread	- Lack of reliability metrics in the implementation
[37]	The number of child node is preserved using Q-learning	Increase stability	- Lesser number of nodes is considered and no real testbed experiments
[38]	Node load, residual energy and ETX	Better Network lifetime and packet delivery ratio	- No real testbed experiments and Lowered stability
[43]	Buffer occupancy, transmission count	Increase network throughput, reduce packet loss and delay	- Consideration of mobility in the network is missing, energy of node is not considered

4   Conclusion

In this paper, we are focusing on the problem of congestion in RPL protocol that occurs when communication is performed in IoT networks. This problem is handled in various ways. One of the major methods is by modifying the RPL protocol to achieve data transmission through a congestion-free route or balance the load in the network effectively. RPL is the standard protocol for Routing in IoT networks. In this survey, we focus on the different approaches of congestion control based on the modification of the RPL protocol.

There are various authors which use the DIO message to send the congestion information to the child node and ask to select the new parent node which is less congested. The value of congestion is calculated based on different parameters that are selected by various authors. The majorly used parameters are ETX, buffer occupancy, and residual energy. There are some authors which perform multipath routing to increase throughput and packet delivery ratio as well achieve better load balancing but they didn't follow the standards of RPL protocol. Priority of the data packet is also considered in some papers but again it changes the frame format and creates a problem of interpretability. One this which is majorly observed that maximum author doesn't consider the mobility of the node which is needed to be considered when it comes to IoT network.

This survey helps to identify the benefits and the limitations of different RPL based approaches for congestion handling. It also helps to decide which kind of approach will be suitable based on the application requirement. It is not simple to say any one of the protocol modifications of RPL is best for routing but there are various approaches presented in this survey that are working well and also maintain their compatibility with native RPL. It is important to modify the native RPL given by RFC need to be modified in the way it can handle the high traffic and also flexible with the situation as well as consider the mobility in the network. This can be done by directly submitting the draft to IETF so that a new version of RPL can be launched and provide the practical model to the researchers.

References

1. Internet of things - number of connected devices worldwide 2015–2025. Technical report, Statista Research Department (2016)
2. Cisco, cisco visual networking index: Forecast and and trends, December 2019
3. Hui, J.W., Culler, D.E.: Extending IP to low-power, wireless personal area networks. IEEE Internet Comput. **12**(4), 37–45 (2008)
4. Ghaleb, B., et al.: A survey of limitations and enhancements of the IPv6 routing protocol for low-power and lossy networks: a focus on core operations. IEEE Commun. Surv. Tutorials **21**(2), 1607–1635 (2018)
5. Abbou, A.N., Baddi, Y., Hasbi, A.: Routing over low power and lossy networks protocol: overview and performance evaluation. In: 2019 International Conference of Computer Science and Renewable Energies (ICCSRE), pp. 1–6. IEEE (2019)
6. Manyika, J., Chui, M., Bisson, P., Woetzel, J., Dobbs, R., Bughin, J., Aharon, D.: The Internet of Things: Mapping the Value Beyond the Hype, vol. 24. McKinsey Global Institute New York, NY, USA (2015)
7. Kharrufa, H., Al-Kashoash, H.A., Kemp, A.H.: RPL-based routing protocols in IoT applications: a review. IEEE Sens. J. **19**(15), 5952–5967 (2019)
8. Pancaroglu, D., Sen, S.: Load balancing for RPL-based internet of things: a review. Ad Hoc Netw. **116**, 102491 (2021)
9. Winter, T., et al.: RPL: Ipv6 routing protocol for low power and lossy networks. draft-ietf-roll-rpl-19 (2011)
10. Thubert, P., et al.: Objective function zero for the routing protocol for low-power and lossy networks (RPL) (2012)
11. Gnawali, O., Levis, P.: The minimum rank with hysteresis objective function. In: RFC 6719, p. 13 (2012)
12. Pister, K., Dejean, N., Barthel, D.: Routing metrics used for path calculation in low-power and lossy networks. RFC **6551** (2012)
13. Levis, P., Clausen, T., Hui, J., Gnawali, O., Ko, J.: The trickle algorithm. Internet Engineering Task Force, RFC6206, pp. 1–13 (2011)
14. Al-Kashoash, H.A., Hassen, F., Kharrufa, H., Kemp, A.H.: Analytical modelling of congestion for 6LoWPAN networks. ICT Express **4**(4), 209–215 (2018)

15. Al-Kashoash, H.A., Kharrufa, H., Al-Nidawi, Y., Kemp, A.H.: Congestion control in wireless sensor and 6LoWPAN networks: toward the internet of things. Wireless Netw. **25**(8), 4493–4522 (2019)
16. Michopoulos, V., Guan, L., Oikonomou, G., Phillips, I.: DCCC6: duty cycle-aware congestion control for 6LoWPAN networks. In: 2012 IEEE International Conference on Pervasive Computing and Communications Workshops, pp. 278–283. IEEE (2012)
17. Castellani, A.P., Rossi, M., Zorzi, M.: Back pressure congestion control for CoAP/6LoWPAN networks. Ad Hoc Netw. **18**, 71–84 (2014)
18. Al-Kashoash, H.A., Hafeez, M., Kemp, A.H.: Congestion control for 6LoWPAN networks: a game theoretic framework. IEEE Internet Things J. **4**(3), 760–771 (2017)
19. Hellaoui, H., Koudil, M.: Bird flocking congestion control for CoAP/RPL/6LoWPAN networks. In: Proceedings of the 2015 Workshop on IoT challenges in Mobile and Industrial Systems, pp. 25–30 (2015)
20. Kim, H.S., Paek, J., Bahk, S.: QU-RPL: queue utilization based RPL for load balancing in large scale industrial applications. In: 2015 12th Annual IEEE International Conference on Sensing, Communication, and Networking (SECON), pp. 265–273. IEEE (2015)
21. Sheu, J.P., Hsu, C.X., Ma, C.: A game theory based congestion control protocol for wireless personal area networks. In: 2015 IEEE 39th Annual Computer Software and Applications Conference, vol. 2, pp. 659–664. IEEE (2015)
22. Ma, C., Sheu, J.P., Hsu, C.X.: A game theory based congestion control protocol for wireless personal area networks. J. Sens. **2016** (2016)
23. Ha, M., Kwon, K., Kim, D., Kong, P.Y.: Dynamic and distributed load balancing scheme in multi-gateway based 6lowpan. In: 2014 IEEE International Conference on Internet of Things (iThings), and IEEE Green Computing and Communications (GreenCom) and IEEE Cyber, Physical and Social Computing (CPSCom), pp. 87–94. IEEE (2014)
24. Tang, W., Ma, X., Huang, J., Wei, J.: Toward improved RPL: a congestion avoidance multipath routing protocol with time factor for wireless sensor networks. J. Sens. **2016** (2016)
25. Lodhi, M.A., Rehman, A., Khan, M.M., Hussain, F.B.: Multiple path RPL for low power lossy networks. In: 2015 IEEE Asia Pacific Conference on Wireless and Mobile (APWiMob), pp. 279–284. IEEE (2015)
26. Al-Kashoash, H.A., Amer, H.M., Mihaylova, L., Kemp, A.H.: Optimization-based hybrid congestion alleviation for 6LoWPAN networks. IEEE Internet Things J. **4**(6), 2070–2081 (2017)
27. Iova, O., Theoleyre, F., Noel, T.: Using multiparent routing in RPL to increase the stability and the lifetime of the network. Ad Hoc Netw. **29**, 45–62 (2015)
28. Qasem, M., Al-Dubai, A., Romdhani, I., Ghaleb, B., Gharibi, W.: A new efficient objective function for routing in internet of things paradigm. In: 2016 IEEE Conference on Standards for Communications and Networking (CSCN), pp. 1–6. IEEE (2016)
29. Nassar, J., Gouvy, N., Mitton, N.: Towards multi-instances QoS efficient RPL for smart grids. In: Proceedings of the 14th ACM Symposium on Performance Evaluation of Wireless Ad Hoc, Sensor, & Ubiquitous Networks, pp. 85–92 (2017)
30. Nassar, J., Berthomé, M., Dubrulle, J., Gouvy, N., Mitton, N., Quoitin, B.: Multiple instances QoS routing in RPL: application to smart grids. Sensors **18**(8), 2472 (2018)

31. Moghadam, M.N., Taheri, H.: High throughput load balanced multipath routing in homogeneous wireless sensor networks. In: 2014 22nd Iranian Conference on Electrical Engineering (ICEE), pp. 1516–1521. IEEE (2014)
32. Ganesan, D., Govindan, R., Shenker, S., Estrin, D.: Highly-resilient, energy-efficient multipath routing in wireless sensor networks. ACM SIGMOBILE Mob. Comput. Commun. Rev. 5(4), 11–25 (2001)
33. Michel, M., Duquennoy, S., Quoitin, B., Voigt, T.: Load-balanced data collection through opportunistic routing. In: 2015 International Conference on Distributed Computing in Sensor Systems, pp. 62–70. IEEE (2015)
34. Nassiri, M., Boujari, M., Azhari, V.: Energy-aware and load-balanced parent selection in RPL routing for wireless sensor networks. Int. J. Wireless Mobile Comput. 9(3), 231–239 (2015)
35. Mamdouh, M., Elsayed, K., Khattab, A.: RPL load balancing via minimum degree spanning tree. In: 2016 IEEE 12th International Conference on Wireless and Mobile Computing, Networking and Communications (WiMob), pp. 1–8. IEEE (2016)
36. Guo, J., Liu, X., Bhatti, G., Orlik, P., Parsons, K.:Load balanced routing for low power and lossy networks, 24 July 2014. US Patent App. 13/746,173
37. Sebastian, A., Sivagurunathan, D.S.: Load balancing optimization for RPL based emergency response using Q-learning. MATTER Int. J. Sci. Technol 4(2), 74–92 (2018)
38. Sankar, S., Srinivasan, P.: Fuzzy logic based energy aware routing protocol for internet of things. Int. J. Intell. Syst. Appl. 10(10), 11 (2018)
39. Gaddour, O., Koubâa, A., Baccour, N., Abid, M.: OF-FL: QoS-aware fuzzy logic objective function for the RPL routing protocol. In: 2014 12th International Symposium on Modeling and optimization in Mobile, Ad Hoc, and Wireless Networks (WiOpt), pp. 365–372. IEEE (2014)
40. Aljarrah, E.: Deployment of multi-fuzzy model based routing in RPL to support efficient IoT. Int. J. Commun. Netw. Inf. Secur. 9(3), 457–465 (2017)
41. Maheshwari, A., Yadav, R.K., Nath, P.: Data congestion control using offloading in IoT network. Wireless Pers. Commun., 1–20 (2022)
42. Maheswari, A., Yadav, R.K., Nath, P.: Data congestion prediction in sensors based IoT network. J. Sci. Ind. Res. (JSIR) 80(12), 1091–1095 (2022)
43. Shreyas, J., Singh, H., Tiwari, S., Srinidhi, N.N., Dilip Kumar, S.M.: CAFOR: congestion avoidance using fuzzy logic to find an optimal routing path in 6lowpan networks. J. Reliable Intell. Environ. 7(4), 325–340 (2021)
44. Liu, X., Guo, J., Bhatti, G., Orlik, P., Parsons, K.: Load balanced routing for low power and lossy networks. In: 2013 IEEE Wireless Communications and Networking Conference (WCNC), pp. 2238–2243. IEEE (2013)
45. Guo, J., Liu, X., Bhatti, G., Orlik, P., Parsons, K.: Load balanced routing for low power and lossy networks, 24 July 2014. US Patent App. 13/746,173

Real Time Dynamic Home Surveillance Using Raspberry Node

G. R. Venkatakrishnan[1], R. Rengaraj[1], R. Jeya[2]([⊠]), Rajalakshmi[2], and K. Sabari Viswanath[1]

[1] Sri Sivasubramaniya Nadar College of Engineering, Kalavakkam, Chennai 603110, India
venkatakrishnangr@ssn.edu.in
[2] SRM Institute of Science and Technology, Kattankalathur, Chennai, India
jeyar@srmist.edu.in

Abstract. Though the modern world is progressive and evolving in many aspects, the foul and evil idea of theft remains intact in the minds of some corrupt people still today. Theft has always been challenging to mankind, right from the days he started to live in houses. To prevent this, he used physical locks, some unbreakable chains, and many other interesting stuffs. Today in the modern world, the securing system are progressive and advanced in many ways with the help of computer technologies, but still the corrupted minds of thieves are tough competitors to all these initiatives. So, in a noble thought of eradicating the theft, we have come up with a modern idea using some electronic components and some great coding algorithms. Our idea is to notify the user (owner of the house) about the presence of persons in front of his/her house during the absence of him. The algorithm we use will differentiate the known and unknown persons of the user. So, whenever there is a presence of unknown person in front of his house, a notification will be sent to the user through a mobile application about the presence.

Keywords: Raspberry pi · PIR sensor · Python · Machine Learning

1 Introduction

Today there are eyes everywhere, and, in thirty years camera surveillance grew from an unknown thing to a necessity in the street, shopping malls, office buildings and factories in transit stations and airports. While such public cameras receive much of the attention, privately owned and operated cameras are even more ubiquitous. Just how densely those cameras are distributed is a matter of some debate. Currently these cameras use Closed-Circuit Television (CCTV) technology, which uses video camera that sends output to a limited set of displaying monitors.

1.1 Closed-Circuit Television and Its Drawbacks

Closed Circuit Television (CCTV) consists of a camera connected by a cable to a display monitor, and these systems provided a minimum level security. These were often

R. Venkataraman et al. (Eds.): ICIoT 2022, CCIS 1727, pp. 14–24, 2023.
https://doi.org/10.1007/978-3-031-28475-5_2

extended to connect up to four cameras to the monitor, the outputs from which could be displayed in a pre-programmed sequence. The cameras were usually stationary. The next addition was to add a video recorder, enabling the monitor to be record the video on a videotape and played back at a later time. One more helpful thing is, the ability of these systems to move the cameras in either the horizontal or vertical plane. These cameras are mostly referred as Pan, Tilt and Zoom (PTZ) cameras.

Though these cameras are helpful in some aspects, they bring the following drawbacks;

- If someone hacks the system, they get to know everything and can do anything.
- Ordinary Surveillance Camera records everything and stores that footage. Basically, it is used to find the victims, and not to prevent the activity.
- Also, most of public Surveillance Cameras are poor in pixel quality.

So, in order to overcome these problems, we have come up with an idea of automatic surveillance using some advanced machine learning concepts.

2 Proposed Plan

Our project is an automated security camera which detects and notify any abnormality to the user. For this we are using a raspberry node, raspberry camera module and a PIR sensor in the hardware part. The machine learning code is done using OpenCV. On embedding both hardware and software, the desired model is achieved. The detailed methodology is as follows.

2.1 Methodology

Initially a Raspberry node, which is connected with a PIR sensor, and a Raspberry camera is placed on a house door facing the outside world. The Raspberry node will be provided with a power supply of 5 V. And now if any movement is observed in the accessible field of the PIR sensor, the sensor will detect it, and provides the output as input to the raspberry camera, which is connected to the raspberry node. Then, within few seconds, the Raspberry camera will capture the image.

Mostly the image captured will be noisy or with low brightness. So, to overcome these difficulties, the captured image will be processed by the machine learning algorithms. And, now the well processed image will be compared with the images of known persons that are already present in the database. Raspberry along with artificial intelligence tools will provide an output based on the comparison. If the processed image is already present in the database, then no output will be generated, if not, then an output with a statement "UNKNOWN FACE DETECTEDNEAR YOUR HOUSE" and the image of unknown person will be sent to the user.

2.2 Flowchart

The flowchart shown in Fig. 1 will clearly explain the complete working of the paper.

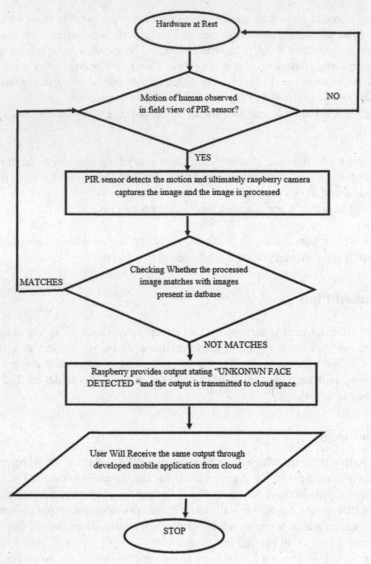

Fig. 1. Working flow of the system

3   Hardware

The prominent hardware products of our project are, raspberry node, raspberry camera module, and PIR sensor.

3.1   PIR Sensor

PIR sensor (Passive Infrared Sensor) shown in Fig. 2 is an electronic sensor which detects infrared radiation emitted by humans. It is also referred to as Motion detector sensor.

The most important factors while selecting the PIR sensor for any application are its time delay and the distance of detection. The time delay is the time period for which the sensor remains high after detecting any motion. The detection distance is the distance up to which the sensor detects motion. The accuracy of selecting PIR sensor based on the two above criteria increases the efficiency of the purpose of using PIR sensor. The prominent purpose to use PIR sensor is to detect the motion of the human beings in the considered surrounding of the setup.

Fig. 2. PIR Sensor

In this project Surveillance camera will be turned ON only when any Human is present. For this PIR Sensor is used. That is when any person comes in the range of PIR Sensor, Raspberry pi camera module interfaced with PIR Sensor gets turned ON.

3.2   Raspberry Node and Raspberry Camera Module

The Raspberry Pi shown in Fig. 3 is similar to a pocket-sized computer. The Raspberry Pi is a microcomputer with dimensions of 9 cm × 5.5 cm. It can do all the things that a desktop does – spreadsheets, word-processing, games and it also plays high-definition video. Raspberry Pi Camera Module shown in Fig. 4 is a Night Vision Camera comes with 3.6 mm Adjustable Focal Length, IR Sensor LED Light 1080P. It can access sensitive lights too. As we seen earlier, PIR Sensor detects any abnormalities and gives it output as input to the connected camera module.

Fig. 3. Raspberry Node   **Fig. 4.** Raspberry Camera Module

3.3 Hardware Specifications

The specifications of the hardware items used in the system is listed in Table 1.

Table 1. Specifications of the hardware items

Component	Specification
Raspberry pi	Version number 4 with 4 gb ram
Raspberry camera module	Night Vision Camera with 3.6 mm Adjustable Focal
PIR sensor	Xcluma HC SR501 HC-SR501 Adjust Infrared

4 Coding and Testing

Our Code uses OpenCV (version 3.4), firebase and face-recognition modules in python. The dataset (Figs. 4 and 5) of desired numbers is collected from the user and then trained. It is then trained and tested to detect the faces other than that in the dataset (Figs. 7 and 8) and stores it in the same path as that of the code. Then the picture is sent to the firebase storage using a python code snippet. It is then reviewed through the app (Fig. 9). The storage bucket and the API key of the firebase storage has to be given to the app to connect to the firebase storage and download the file. The coding is divided into three parts;

4.1 Adding User Faces to the Database (Code and Output)

The code for adding user faces in the database is given below and output for the same is shown in Figs. 5 and 6.

BEGIN
  Import cv2, os
  Declare haarcascade classifier as facedetect
  Set img_id TO 0
  Declare user_id
  Get user_id From user
  While TRUE Start
      Declare check, img
      Check if the video is read
      Convert the img into gray scale
      Declare faces
      Define scale factor and min neighbours in the
             detecTMultiscale Attribute
      For face detected
         Start
             Outline rectangle for the face detected
            · Write the image in a folder name "FACES"
             Increment img_id
             Show the Frame
        End IF
      End While
      Release/Stop Video
END

Fig. 5. Adding user data to the database

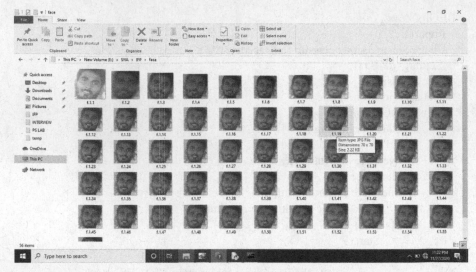

Fig. 6. Storing the user data

4.2 Training the Node Using the Given Data (Code and Output)

The pseudo code for training the data is given below and output for the same is shown in Figs. 7.

```
BEGIN
    Import cv2, os,numpy
    SET path TO "FACES"
    Declare haarcascade classifier as facedetect
    Declare facerecognizer as clf
    Declare faces,ids
     Set Faces,ids TO Function train_classifier WITH path as
        PARAMETER
Train the recognizer with Faces,ids
Write in "classifier.yml"
FUNCTION train_classifier START
    Declare lists facesamples, ids
    From path retrieve images as img
    For face detected in img START
        SET facesamples with the boundaries of the face
        SET ids to the id of the face
END FOR
Return facesamples,ids
END
```

Fig. 7. Training the data

4.3 Detecting and Capturing Unknown Faces (Code and Output)

The pseudo code for detecting and capturing unknown faces is given below and output for the same is shown in Figs. 8 and 9.

```
BEGIN
    Import cv2, os,numpy
    Declare haarcascade classifier as facedetect
    While TRUE Start
            Declare check,img
            Check if the video is read
            Convert the img into gray scale
            Declare faces
            Define scale factor and min neighbours in the
                    detecTMultiscale Attribute
            For face detected
                Start
                    Outline rectangle for the face detected
                    Declare id, confidence
                    SET id,confidence TO Predicted face using the
                            recognizer clf
                    IF confidence is less than the Threshold value
                        START IF
                            It is a Known Face
                        END IF
                    ELSE
                        START ELSE
                            It is an unknown Face
```

WRITE the img to the folder
END ELSE
End FOR
Show the Frame
End While
Release/Stop Video
END

Fig. 8. Detecting the known face

Fig. 9. Detecting the unknown face

4.4 Viewing the Output Through Mobile Application

The output shown in Figs. 8 and 9 can also be viewed using mobile application as shown in Fig. 10.

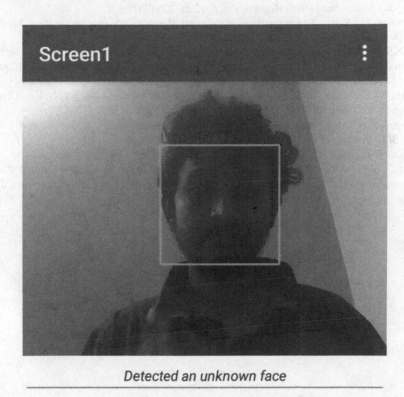

Fig. 10. Receiving unknown face in mobile app

In this way, the user can be able to get known of the unknown persons near his house. This code will be efficient in such a way that, the user can be notified within few minutes about this activity.

5 Conclusion

The output of the proposed system will be a useful product to both the users and the society. This paper is based on the Raspberry pi, OpenCV and python. These platforms are Free Open-Source Software, so the overall cost of the product will also be low. This paper will result in a commercial product which provides surveillance for homes, and if extended further home automation can be implemented using this face recognizing method. So, the overall implementation cost is low and can be easily configured. More importantly, the proposed system, can be accessed anywhere across the globe, and the serious threat of theft can be eliminated for forever.

References

1. Huang, G.B., Lee, H., Miller, E.L.: Learning hierarchical representation for face verification with convolution deep belief networks. In: Proceedings of International Conference on Computer Vision and Pattern Recognition, pp. 223–226 (2012)
2. Makwana, H., Singh, T.: Comparison of different algorithm for face recognition. Global J. Comput. Sci. Technol. Graph. Vis. **13**(9) (2013)
3. Tathe, S.V., Narote, A.S., Narote, S.P.: Human face detection and recognition in video. In: International Conference on Advances in Computing Communications and Informatics (ICACCI) (2016)
4. Swathi, V., Fernandes, S.: Raspberry Pi based human face detection. Int. J. Adv. Res. Comput. Commun. Eng. **4**(9) (2015)
5. Georgescu, D.: A real-time face recognition system using eigenfaces. J. Mob. Embed. Distrib. Syst. **3**(4) (2011)
6. Abaya, W.F., Basa, J., Sy, M., Abad, A.C., Dadios, E.P.: Low cost smart security camera with night vision capability using Raspberry Pi and OpenCV. In: International Conference on Humanoid Nanotechnology Information Technology Communication and Control Environment and Management (HNICEM), pp. 1–6 (2014)

NEORS - Novel Efficient and Optimal Resource Scheduling Technique for Cloud Infrastructure Services

S. Peer Mohamed Ziyath[1] , S. Senthilkumar[2](✉), R. Rajkumar[3] ,
and C. M. Arun Kumar[4]

[1] Department of Computer Applications, B.S. Abdur Rahman Crescent Institute of Science and
Technology, Chennai, India
[2] CSE, University College of Engineering, Pattukkottai, India
senthilucepkt@gmail.com
[3] DSBS, SRM Institute of Science and Technology, Chennai, India
[4] ECE, University College of Engineering, Pattukkottai, India

Abstract. The cloud computing technique is a combination of web services and
virtualization technology. Cloud gives dynamism, vulnerability and versatility
based administrations to clients in pay-more only as costs arise style over the
web. For virtualized record participation in cloud foundation, distributed computing employs booking and burden adjusting. These two things must be done in
an advanced way in a distributed computing environment to get the best use of
resources. In late decade, increment in demands (various and complex applications) for cloud administrations is bringing the remaining task at hand up in cloud
condition. The purpose of this research work is to develop a technique which could
handle the dynamic nature of the attributes of the submitted tasks. In this connection, NEORS technique is proposed. The proposed technique consists of two sub
algorithms for handling dynamic user attribute request and dynamic attribute values during the execution of tasks. Simulations were led to assess the viability
utilizing Cloudsim test system in cloud server farms and results represents that
this implementation achieves better execution as far as resource allocation efficiency, average rate, task allocation and task completion time than the existing
strategies.

Keywords: Resource scheduling · Cloud services · Optimization · IaaS
Services · Virtualization

1 Introduction

With the expansion in the client base and the interest for the cloud framework, a few
organizations have likewise begun to offer the assistance [3]. Clients can get to different
sorts of administrations from cloud like asset pooling, versatile and adaptable [2], adaptability [1], utility administrations, throughput, execution, high accessibility, overseen
administrations and so forth because of brought together administration of cloud foundation. The fundamental thought behind the asset provisioning is to identify and choose

R. Venkataraman et al. (Eds.): ICIoT 2022, CCIS 1727, pp. 25–34, 2023.
https://doi.org/10.1007/978-3-031-28475-5_3

the best assets for clients dependent on up and coming application demand (requests), so up and coming interest can get an ideal asset for example Number of assets expected to serve the application ought to be least to keep up an alluring degree of administration quality (least execution time and greatest throughput). Asset booking demonstrates how assets can be distributed among a variety of cloud users in accordance with predetermined policies and guidelines for asset utilization in a given cloud environment. Asset provisioning associates upcoming solicitations with running virtual machines, ensuring that the client receives administrations at the lowest possible cost and in the shortest possible time, while the specialist organization receives the maximum benefit without jeopardizing SLA compliance [7]. In this situation, a proficient asset booking and burden adjusting stay the significant part to be focused for effective document distribution. The majority of the exploration works have been created for asset booking and burden adjusting in the cloud. Assi et al. [4], for instance, tended to adaptable traffic the executives (STM) in the cloud using a new disintegration approach. The most extreme connection load was discovered to be reduced with the help of STM, ensuring load balancing between clients in the organization. According to this issue, an adaptable remaining task at hand driven apportioning plan was introduced by Ahirrao and Ingle [5] targeting enhancing the reaction time and throughput for disseminated exchanges. Dhinesh Babu L.D. et al. [6] used Honey Bee behavior to gain insight into task planning for cloud conditions. Searching conduct of bumble bees are utilized to viably adjust the heap across VM in a cloud situation. In this research work, to address the issues discussed above, a novel efficient and optimal resource scheduling technique is proposed for allocation of virtual machines during runtime according to the user requirements. The remaining part of the paper is organized as follows: Sect. 2 discusses a few existing scheduling techniques as well as their disadvantages. Section 3 describes the proposed efficient and optimal resource scheduling technique, while Sect. 4 depicts the proposed technique's performance evaluation in comparison to a few existing techniques discussed in Sect. 2. Section 5 of the paper concludes with suggestions for future research.

2 Related Work

In [9], the authors examine how well the QoS booking calculation works with makespan, idleness, load balancing, and cost factor. In [10], the authors proposed a booking procedure for distributed computing assets that was based on the boundaries of cost, trust, and time, as well as other factors. The calculation is proper for asset booking and gives high effectiveness in enormous scope distributed computing. In [11], the authors proposed and implemented two planning calculations for errand booking: the Shortest Cloudlet Fastest Processing Element (SCFP) and the Longest Cloudlet Fastest Processing Element (LCFP). Calculations mirror the handling limitation of an undertaking and the computational ability of an asset during the booking appraisals measure. The entire makespan to achieve the assignments are utilized as the measurement to figure the results of the recommended calculations. The authors of [12] suggested calculations based on the capacities of all virtual machines (VMs), the duration of all mentioned activities, and the interdependence of numerous errands. Dissimilar assets constrained by appointing undertakings to appropriate assets through dynamic booking or static booking and increment the client fulfillment level. In any circumstance, security is one of the primary issues in cloud environment stayed unaddressed. In [13], the authors proposed a min-max booking calculation that assigned the largest errands to the best assets first to improve make span time, reaction time, and asset utilization as a percentage of client demand. However, the calculation encountered issues with asset overutilization and underutilization and failed to improve required boundaries. The creators of [14, 15] proposed a few improved forms of max-min calculation to upgrade the QoS boundaries in distributed computing, but the proposed calculations failed to improve the key presentation marker boundaries. In [16], the creators built up the differential count technique was utilized to reproduce the ideal dynamic VM asset sets. Test results exhibited that the presentation of the calculation is acceptable, however its computational expenses were high. The creators of [17, 18] proposed techniques which took numerous elements, for example, VM assets and organization data transmission into thought, and improved the conventional closeout instrument a ton. A proficient and reliable asset sharing stage was examined in [19] utilizing multi-QoS-arranged asset determination and cost helped asset control for synergistic distributed computing. In [20], a Collaborative Protocol (CProtocol) was described to reduce irregularity during asset booking by utilising novel burden adjusting heuristics. The authors of [21] developed a Fuzzy-based Multidimensional Resource Scheduling model for cloud asset planning productivity. In [22], the authors developed a strategy to address the issue of virtual machine (VM) planning for distributed computing by introducing a novel versatile VM asset booking calculation dependent up for sale component that takes into account a variety of factors such as network transmission capacity and closeout cutoff time. The authors of [23] proposed a Multi-Resource Scheduling Algorithm for Hybrid Cloud-Based Large-Scale Media Streaming to efficiently deliver a large amount of media content using a topographically circulated half breed cloud (MHLMS). The above discussed methods are not optimal for resource scheduling under dynamic constraints provided by the user during requirements submission. To overcome these issues in this paper we have proposed a novel efficient and optimal resource scheduling technique inspired by fuzzy and nature based optimization algorithms.

3 NEORS Technique

In the proposed technique, the planning calculation is responsible for distributing the multidimensional assets (for example Processor, Memory and Bandwidth). With the target of greatest asset use and least preparing time, booking of assets as indicated by client demands in an equal manner and burden adjusting of the planned assets is the issue to be explained in this paper. So as to tackle this issue (for example most extreme asset use and least handling time), this proposes a planning calculation dependent on the user given attribute values and runtime attribute values of virtual machines in cloud cluster. A Directed Acyclic Graph (DAG) is used to represent an equal application consisting of assets to be planned during the asset portion. The vertices of the DAG represent the cloud client's parceled assets, while the edges represent the connections between the assets. The relation between tasks and resources are represented as

$$Ex(Tn) = op.Al(\int_1^n STm, \ VMr) \tag{1}$$

where, STm defines the sub tasks of each task submitted by the user ranging from 1 to n, VMr defines the virtual machines of the infrastructure ranging from 1 to r. Ex(Tn) defines the execution of the task T ranging from 1 to n. The successful execution of the tasks depends on optimal allocation of virtual machines to the sub tasks of task T. The NEORS technique is designed to reduce total waiting time and improve resource scheduling efficiency for each cloud user resource request. In Fig. 1, the architecture of the proposed method is depicted.

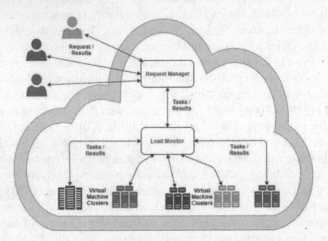

Fig. 1. Architecture of NEORS

The components of the architecture are Request manager, and Load monitor. Request manager is the agent which is responsible for receiving request from the users initially and also during runtime of process. The requests are made up of attributes like CPU, memory, bandwidth, operating system, storage etc. these attribute values are given by the user during request submission. The user is permitted to ask for more attribute values in the middle of the process execution. The initial request is defined as follows

$$IREQ\ (Tn) = \int_{1}^{n} \{A1,\ A2,\ \ldots.,\ An\} \tag{2}$$

where IREQ(Tn) defines the initial request for all the tasks ranging from 1 to n. The corresponding attribute values required are given as A1, A2, ... An. The integral part of all the tasks is taken into account. During the runtime user may ask for higher value of attributes to be allocated for a specific task. The representation of the runtime request is given as follows

$$DREQ(Tx) = \{A1,\ Ae,\ Ah,\ \ldots.Az\} \tag{3}$$

where DREQ(Tx) defines the updated dynamic request of a particular task Tx. The corresponding attribute values required are given as A1, Ae, Ah, ..., Az. The dynamic attribute value along with the corresponding task Tx will be received by the request manager and forward it to load monitor for resource allocation. The load monitor checks for the current capacity of the VM handling the Tx and if it is lesser than the requested value then the load monitor will move the task to a new VM with requested attribute values. The entire process is depicted in algorithm I given in Table 1.

Table 1. User Attribute based Resource Scheduling.

Start
Input: Set of Tasks 1 to n
          Corresponding attributes A1, A2, …… An of each task T
Output: $Ex(Tn) = op.Al(\int_1^n STm, VMr)$
          STm is sub tasks if task T and VM is virtual machine
Initialize
          $IREQ\ (Tn) = \int_1^n \{A1, A2, …., An\}$
Request Manager assigns VM as
For all T from 1 to n
          $VMx \longleftarrow \cup_1^n T\{A1, A2, ….., An\}x$
Dynamic submission
          $DREQ(Tx) = \{A1, Ae, Ah, …. Az\}$
Load monitor assigns VM as
For all T from 1 to x
    If current $VM(\sum_1^n A) > T(\sum_1^x A)$ no change in VM
    Else
              $VMx \longleftarrow \int_1^n T\{A1, A2, ……, An\}x$
Continue until all task executed
End

The above attribute based resource scheduling is depending upon the attribute values submitted by user at initial stage as well as runtime. During the runtime if the user changes the attribute values, then the load monitor will look for the new virtual machine if the current virtual machine attribute values do not match the requirements. The attribute values are summed to match the required values and Virtual machine with higher than that value will be assigned newly for the current running task. The above algorithm is best suitable only when the user submits the new attribute values. But there are certain times where the current running task may need higher attribute values like more memory, bandwidth etc. due to the internal process of the task. In that case the above said algorithm is not optimal, so we have developed a variant of this algorithm which is called as Runtime attribute based resource scheduling algorithm. This algorithm could handle the runtime changes and requirements in new attribute values. During the runtime the load monitor will monitor the progress of the task execution in each virtual machines and if in any of the virtual machines resources like memory, CPU etc. are exceeding the threshold limit then the load monitor will find the input level of the current task for last few sections. If the last few sections are submitting tasks and utilizing the resources more than threshold of the resources, then the load monitor will assign a new virtual machine with double the value of the current attribute values so that the new virtual machine could handle the submitted tasks effectively and continue the workflow by keeping the service level agreement honored. The entire runtime based resource scheduling is given in algorithm II as Table 2.

Table 2. Runtime based Resource Scheduling.

start
Input: Set of Tasks 1 to n
              Corresponding attributes A1, A2, ... An of each task T
Output: $Ex(Tn) = op.Al(\int_1^n STm, VMr)$
              STm is sub tasks if task T and VM is virtual machine
Initialize
              $IREQ\ (Tn) = \int_1^n\{A1, A2, ..., An\}$
Request Manager assigns VM as
For all T from 1 to n
              $VMx \longleftarrow \cup_1^n T\{A1, A2, ..., An\}x$
Runtime verification
For all T from 1 to x
      If current $T(\sum_1^n\{A1, A2, ..., An\}) \geq Th\{An\}$ then
          If past $(\frac{1}{3})\sum_1^n\{A1, A2, ..., An\} \geq (1/2)Th\{An\}$ then
                          $VMx \longleftarrow 2 * (\int_1^n T\{A1, A2, ..., An\}x)$
      Else
                      continue
Continue until all task executed
End

As per the algorithm II, the load monitor monitors the progress of the execution of tasks in virtual machines. If any of the attribute values of the virtual machine exceeds the threshold for a particular time period then the last few sections of execution is checked for its attributes values. If one third of the attribute values exceeds the half of the threshold value then the virtual machine is assumed to be exceeding its execution capacity and a new virtual machine with double the value of the previous attribute values assigned for continuing the execution of the tasks.

4 Performance Evaluation

For any newly proposed techniques, it is necessary to measure the performance of the technique in terms of well-known parameters and compare it with few existing solutions. For this NEORS technique, for performance evaluation, the parameters taken into consideration are average success rate, resource scheduling efficiency, task completion time and task allocation time. The performance is compare with the following existing methods: RSL [21], VMRS [22], and MHLMS [23]. So as to check the viability of the proposed method, we pick the CloudSim [24] programming to finish the investigations. The stage is a personal computer whose specifications are as per the following: 2.4 GHz CPU, 16 GB Memory, 1000 GB storage. Those values are fixed for static simulation and minimum for dynamic simulation, but can be increased during runtime for both. The proposed technique's performance is compared to other methods in terms of average success rate in Fig. 2. Figure 3 proves that the proposed NEORS technique outperforms other techniques.

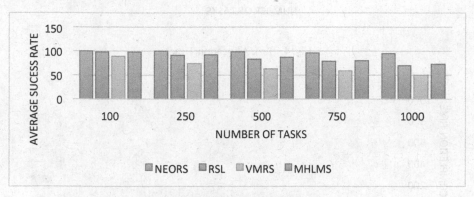

Fig. 2. Average Success Rate

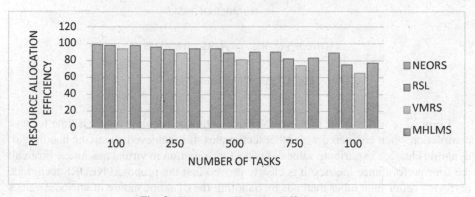

Fig. 3. Resource Allocation Efficiency.

Figure 4 provides information about the performance comparison in terms of task allocation time (in seconds). Task allocation time is the time required for moving the tasks from request manager to the virtual machines for execution of tasks. When compared to other methods, the proposed NEORS technique takes less time to assign tasks to virtual machines (see Fig. 4). Figure 5 shows a comparison of the proposed technique to other methods in terms of task completion time (in seconds).

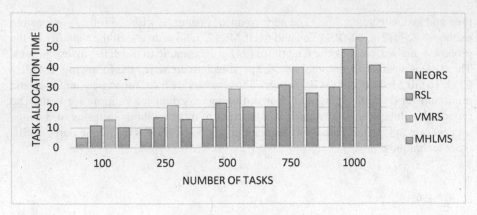

Fig. 4. Task Allocation Time.

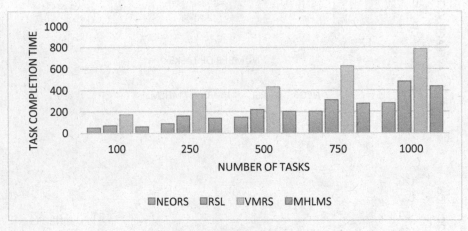

Fig. 5. Task Completion Time.

Figure 5 proves that the proposed NEORs technique requires very less time for task completion when compared with other techniques. It is achieved due to the handling of dynamic changes in attribute values of tasks for execution in virtual machines. From all the four performance metrics, it is clearly proved that the proposed NEORS technique performs better than other methods by handling the dynamic nature of attribute values and thus require less time for task allocation as well as task completion.

5 Conclusion

The proposed technique consists of two sub algorithms where first algorithm is user attribute based scheduling algorithm and second one is runtime based scheduling algorithm. The first algorithm takes the initial and dynamic attribute values submitted by user and schedules the resources accordingly. The second algorithm monitors the current running tasks and if any of the task attribute values exceeds the threshold, it automatically allocates new virtual machine for meeting the demand and continue the execution of tasks. This dynamic nature of the proposed technique makes it providing optimal scheduling for infrastructure services and the performance evaluation also proves that. As the current dynamic nature may allocate the more resources for continuously varying attribute based tasks, the future research will address the issue and new modified technique based on NEORS will be proposed

References

1. Kumar, M., Sharma, S.C.: Deadline constrained based dynamic load balancing algorithm with elasticity in cloud environment. J. Comput. Electr. Eng. (CAEE) **69**, 395–411 (2017). https://doi.org/10.1016/j.compeleceng.2017.11.018
2. Kumar, M., Dubey, K., Sharma, S.C.: Elastic and flexible deadline constraint load balancing algorithm for cloud computing. In: 6th International Conference on Smart Computing and Communications, India, pp. 717–724 (2018)
3. Armbrust, M., et al.: Above the clouds: a Berkeley view of cloud computing, February 2009
4. Assi, C., Ayoubi, S., Sebbah, S., Shaban, K.: Towards scalable traffic management in cloud data centers. IEEE Trans. Commun. **62**(3), 1033–1045 (2014)
5. Ahirrao, S., Ingle, R.: Scalable transactions in cloud data stores. J. Cloud Comput. **4**(1), 1–14 (2015). https://doi.org/10.1186/s13677-015-0047-3
6. Dhinesh Babu, L.D., Venkata Krishna, P.: Honey bee behavior inspired load balancing of tasks in cloud computing environments. Appl. Soft Comput. **13**, 2292–2303 (2013)
7. Javadi, B., et al.: Hybrid cloud resource provisioning policy in the presence of resource failures. In: 4th International Conference on Cloud Computing Technology and Science, CloudCom, pp. 10–17 (2012)
8. Jennings, B., Stadler, R.: Resource management in clouds: survey and research challenges. J. Netw. Syst. Manag. 1–53 (2014)
9. Bansal, N., Maurya, A., Kumar, T., Singh, M., Bansal, S.: Cost performance of QoS driven task scheduling in cloud computing. Proc. Comput. Sci. **57**, 126–130 (2015)
10. Zhong-Wen, G., Kai, Z. The research on cloud computing resource scheduling method based on time cost trust model. In: 2012 2nd International Conference on Computer Science and Network Technology (ICCSNT), pp. 939–942. IEEE (2012)
11. Sindhu, S., Mukherjee, S.: Efficient task scheduling algorithms for cloud computing environment. In: Mantri, A., Nandi, S., Kumar, G., Kumar, S. (eds.) HPAGC 2011. CCIS, vol. 169, pp. 79–83. Springer, Heidelberg (2011). https://doi.org/10.1007/978-3-642-22577-2_11
12. Chitra Devi, D., Rhymend Uthariaraj, V.: Load balancing in cloud computing environment using improved weighted round robin algorithm for non-preemptive dependent tasks. Sci. World J. **2016**, 1–14 (2016)
13. Chen, H., Wang, F., Helian, N., Akanmu, G.: User priority guided Min-Min scheduling algorithm for load balancing in cloud computing. In: National Conference on Parallel Computing Technologies (PARCOMPTECH), Bangalore, India, October 2013
14. Kanani, B., Maniyar, B.: Review on max-min task scheduling algorithm for cloud computing. J. Emerg. Technol. Innov. Res. **2**(3) (2015)
15. Li, X., et al.: An improved max-min task-scheduling algorithm for elastic cloud. In: International Symposium on Computer, Consumer and Control (IS3C), pp. 340–343 (2014)
16. Hu, Z.J.: The Resource Availability Evaluation in Service Grid Environment for QoS. Central South University, Changsha (2010)

17. Zaman, S., Grosu, D.: Combinatorial auction-based allocation of virtual machine instances in clouds. J. Parallel Distrib. Comput. **73**(4), 495–508 (2013)
18. Liu, X., Yuan, C.W., Yang, Z., et al.: VM dynamic scheduling algorithm for mobile cloud computing. Syst. Eng. Electron. **37**(9), 2176–2181 (2015)
19. Shen, H., Liu, G.: An efficient and trustworthy resource sharing platform for collaborative cloud computing. IEEE Trans. Parallel Distrib. Syst. **25**(4), 862–875 (2014)
20. Gutierrez-Garcia, J.O., Ramirez-Nafarrate, A.: Collaborative agents for distributed load management in cloud data centers using live migration of virtual machines. IEEE Trans. Serv. Comput. **8**(6), 916–929 (2015)
21. Priya, V., Kumar, C.S., Kannan, R.: Resource scheduling algorithm with load balancing for cloud service provisioning. Appl. Soft Comput. **76** (2019). https://doi.org/10.1016/j.asoc.2018.12.021
22. Kong, W., Lei, Y., Ma, J.: Virtual machine resource scheduling algorithm for cloud computing based on auction mechanism. Optik **127**(12) (2016). https://doi.org/10.1016/j.ijleo.2016.02.061
23. Liu, Y., Wei, W., Xu, H.: Efficient multi-resource scheduling algorithm for hybrid cloud-based large-scale media streaming. Comput. Electr. Eng. **75** (2019). https://doi.org/10.1016/j.compeleceng.2019.02.007
24. Calheiros, R.N., Ranjan, R., Beloglazov, A., De Rose, C.A.F., Buyya, R.: CloudSim: a toolkit for modeling and simulation of cloud computing environments and evaluation of resource provisioning algorithms. Softw.: Pract. Exp. (SPE) **41**(1), 23–50 (2011). ISSN 0038-0644

Identification of Traffic Signs for the Prevention of Road Accidents Using Convolution Neural Network

T. Primya[1(✉)], G. Kanagaraj[2], G. Subashini[3], R. Divakar[4], and B. Vishnupriya[1]

[1] KPR Institute of Engineering and Technology, Coimbatore, India
primyacse@gmail.com
[2] Kumaraguru College of Technology, Coimbatore, India
[3] PSG College of Technology, Coimbatore, India
[4] Bannari Amman Institute of Technology, Sathyamangalam, India

Abstract. Road signs control traffic, provide traffic guidelines, inform drivers about directions, and warn drivers of dangerous locations. Traffic Sign Detection and Recognition (TSDR) is crucial in this case since it detects and recognizes a sign, alerting the motorist to any subsequent signs. Drivers will no longer have to strain to grasp what the sign signifies thanks to this Advanced Driver Assistance Systems (ADAS) application. There is a need to make the road safer as the population grows and the demand for vehicles grows. With the growing request for automobile intelligence, it's vital to employ computer technology to recognize people automatically and detect traffic signs. A convolutional neural network model was created in the proposed system to categorize traffic indicators into different kinds. This model will allow to recite and comprehend traffic signs, which is an important responsibility for each and every vehicle.

Keywords: Advanced Driver Assistance Systems (ADAS) application · Traffic Sign Detection and Recognition (TSDR) · Image Equalization · Sign Recognition

1 Introduction

15 years ago, innovation was a buzzword, but now a new age is being explored. Many automotive development companies already have Advanced Driving Assistance Systems (ADAS). Car development businesses built a powerful map that helps automobiles navigate using GPS and Internet connections. These technologies are still in their infancy and are undergoing significant transformations. There are numerous flaws in this technology that have not yet been addressed in all vehicles. This feature is only available on high-end, imported vehicles. These are capable of navigating in the counted and tested areas, but updating the map is not possible when a vehicle enters an unidentified location or has problems connecting to the Internet, leaving the car to fix its personal entity. This can result in a variety of issues, including lateness or even loss. To address these issues, a smart system with a camera supply that can watch and recognize traffic signals is required. Individuals will no longer need to look at problems that occur more

frequently since they can now attempt to solve problems that have not yet occurred but may happen in the future, much like a researcher. There are plenty excellent prospects for new shows, and techpreneurs must fill the need. Knowing what not to do allows you to remain a safe distance from the blunders and focus on the tasks at hand. As a result, traffic signal recognition was carried out, which could be used in conjunction with any vehicle to detect various impending road signs.

2 Objectives

The major objective is to create a method for locating road signs. When a camera in a car takes a picture of a complex region, this technology can help resident or nation-wide authorities uphold and update traffic and traffic signals by inevitably detecting and separating one or more road signs. When a traffic signal is spotted, the system uses the CNN algorithm to try to identify the sign and presents the outcome of the separation. It is attempting to develop a warning system that can alert drivers of oncoming traffic signs ahead of time in order to avoid road accidents.

3 Scope of the Paper

To have a better understanding of the characteristics of roads and road signs, as well as the consequences for using imagery in the recognition job. In a transformation such as translating, rotating, or measuring based on invariant shape formats, creating a consistent identifier is important. Identify the best method for extracting a characteristic from traffic signs. Create a road sign classification algorithm that works. Evaluate the performance of existing sturdiness methods under a variety of weather situations and lighting geometries.

4 Literature Survey

This study has presented a variety of methods for refining the correctness of the road sign identification system, automatic detection while reducing the number of supporting vectors required, lowering memory requirements and reducing the time required to test new samples [1]. The presented extension is a good method to improve the system's accuracy while also slightly avoiding illumination variations in the signals to be detected. Although histogram measurement enhances accuracy, there are more pre-processing picture operations to compare than there are when comparing stretch.

Other solutions are implemented to increase accuracy and diminish the quantity of supporting vectors once indicators have been examined in advance. The first of these techniques involves tweaking hyperparameters, which are critical to SVM performance, by employing particle swarm optimization to achieve faster search than grid testing and enabling hyperparameter adjustment with a function that minimizes error and support vectors. This approach is expanded to include every binary separator's parameter as well as character training for other binary dividers. Finally, by gathering those service providers near enough together, more reductions in the number of supported vectors can be obtained. Using vector support equipment, 95.5% segmentation is obtained. There are

36,000 Spanish traffic lights in database, separated into 193 sign classifications. Though, it's questionable if the training and evaluation sets are truly independent, given that the random assignment was solely for the sake of maintaining road sign class allocation. This database is not accessible to the general public.

This research proposes a novel approach to image representation and the selection of discriminatory geographical features, which is demonstrated to be useful in the gratitude of road signs [2]. It has been demonstrated that, in addition to discrete-color picture representation, metric distance based on Color Distance Transform, and the enhanced feature selection procedure, detailed character descriptions may be built from appropriate templates based on one- vs—all distinct permutations. Standard separation can compete with contemporary approaches, processing sequences of input videos virtually in real time, using these available definitions. For starters, feature releases are done straight from publicly signed template images, which makes training less successful than data-driven methods like AdaBoost. Next, each template is treated uniquely, as seen by the quantity, placement, and relevance of local areas issued in order to meet the desired amount of variety, which is determined globally from the other templates. Finally, CDT shown that, while being based on pure template images, the suggested signal description is suitable for modelling the diversity of traffic signals observed in audio and video. The entire system detects and classifies 48 different signals with an accuracy of 85.3% while detecting severity error rates of less than 9%.

The outcomes of many tests are accessible in this report. The expansion of neural networks for sign separation is still incomplete, and a few categories are known: Signs of a bond, a block, or a yield. The tests are carried out in a variety of locations and under various lighting conditions [3]. Every frame is separated into two lines: the top row displays all of the symbols discovered in that frame in 50 by 50 pixels, while the bottom row displays all of the relevant symbol kinds separated. All forms of signs are highly received, if a little perplexing at times. Signs are visible in general once they are very adjacent to the vehicle (e.g., 20 m) and seem to be unsuited with the camera; for example, a yield login changing view does not allow the Programme to find, whereas the identical symbol is appropriately recognized. Signs can be spotted up to 30 m in advance of time, according to royal tests. This distance can be raised to shorten the camera room, but you'll miss out on the chance to obtain closer and closer to the car. Because the neural net supplied for this class has yet to be established, all kinds of indications are well classified without any notable signs. The entire system detects and classifies 48 different signals with an accuracy of 85.3% while detecting severity error rates of less than 9%. Various methods for detecting and distinguishing traffic signals have been covered in this work [4].

The recognition is based on the use of histogram of histogram oriented (HOG) characteristics to reduce vector machine filters (SVM). The technology is precise for high-speed vehicles, works in a variety of weather situations, and runs at a rate of 20 frames per second on average. Color and form analysis are included in the discovery module. SVM partition, an edge detection that improves results, is included in the partition module. The system must be able to provide the best outcomes in order to improve accuracy. This research outlined a strategy for detecting and classifying fast rectangular signals in the United States [5].

A mono grayscale camera with a resolution of 700×400 pixels is used in the system. Video data can be treated in real time on a dual laptop running at 2.16 GHz. Speed signals may be obtained at 27 frames per second, whereas detecting, tracking, and establishing speed signals requires 11 frames per second. In an 11-min sample video with 80 instant signals, the total detection rate was 98.75%, with one false alarm per 42 s, and the separation rate was 97. %, resulting in a total recognition rate of 96.25%. 2880 photos were used to train a number-based speed restriction. In 1233 photos, it achieves a 92.4% accuracy ratio. Though, photos of the same road sign are shared between sets is unclear. With two types of similar international structures working in accordance with the US and EU symbols, both of which have a 90% correct signal detection rate, this research offered a robust and effective technique for detecting the acquisition and recognition limit [6].

Only raw videos are required, and the system can process real-time video streaming of 640×480 pixels at 20 frames per second on a basic 2.13 GHz computer. It takes relatively low number of false alarms E. coli is abundant. The system tests described in this study were not allowed to be recorded on French highways and streets. Experiments are currently underway in other EU nations where sign digits are often considerably different. As long as the ODR neural network is trained in a database with examples of all the needed digital types, the results will be satisfactory. Furthermore, the results presented in this research are only for daylight work. The night and night programme, on the other hand, is currently undergoing a performance evaluation, which is quite encouraging. On 281 road signs, the suggested approach achieves 89% US performance and 90% European speed restrictions, respectively, when including detection and tracking. The results of individual segmentation are not provided.

The content of each traffic sign is extracted and informed using low-level computers, flexible, and accurate approaches in this paper [7].

Binarization, region of interest (ROI), and pixel division have all stood demonstrated to be fruitful strategies and approaches for identifying traffic signals. Depending on a range of circumstances such as the angle of the collected image, day, night, and so on, the system has been shown to generate high precision detection. According to tests, normal visibility can reach up to 35% of occluded traffic signs. Honesty is a critical component in practice. However, learning to read a traffic sign can be tough, just like learning to recognize an object in a natural setting where lighting conditions fluctuate with the weather. Access is also hampered by occurrence of supplementary items on the scene, like moving cars, bicycles, pedestrians, and business signs. The hue of road signs is changed by prolonged exposure to sunlight and its reaction. Because of blurring of movement and vibration of the vehicle, photographs taken in a moving car have a lower image quality. As a result, obtaining genuine road signs from these forums becomes extremely difficult.

A new real-time road sign system and a monitoring system were described in this research [8].

Color, shape, and movement are all included in the programme. It consist of three primary parts such as a well-known colour acquisition framework, a fast-paced Hough-like conversion, an independent country recognition module. The outcomes reported in studies reveal low accuracy; nonetheless, this is a direct outcome of extensive test-ing in a variety of countries, weather conditions, seasons, and other environmental circumstances.

A traffic sign detection system and a sign detection system on a provided image to a car camera were discussed in this work [9]. The three steps of image analysis are usually detection, segmentation, classification. The sign is located on the edge and is used to distinguish rear mark. When two GTSRB and GTSDB data sets are used for traffic sign detection and recognition, the system recommends simplifying functionality. Many forms of complicated road signs like landmarks, uneven lighting, traffic signs with distortion, closures, similar background colours, in addition to real-time maps, are included in these data sets.

5 Problem Definition

Traffic signs are regions of the road that use words or signs to convey, direct, restrict, warn, or instruct information. Almost everything in today's society is made easier by default. Drivers frequently ignore traffic board signs on the sidewalks in an effort to focus on the road, which can be dangerous for them and others. Another typical issue is a lack of understanding of the sign's significance. Every year, car accidents are a leading cause of death, injury, and property damage. These signals might also be missed while travelling at high speeds. The average mortality rate in India was 17.4 fatalities per 100,000 people. The driver must pay close attention to road signs. Road accidents may occur if vehicles and pedestrians fail to observe road signs. Road signs direct traffic, provide traffic directions, inform drivers of directions, and warn drivers of dangerous locations. There is a need to make the road safer as the population grows and the demand for vehicles grows. With the growing demand for automobile intelligence, it's critical to use computer technology to identify road signs automatically. This difficulty can be avoided if there is a reliable mechanism to inform the driver without diverting his or her attention away from the road. This proposed approach is an effective solution for the Road Signs Recognition System to overcome this difficulty.

6 Proposed System

The suggested system comprises of a Traffic Sign Recognition system based on convo-lutional neural networks that has the highest accuracy of all 43 classes. The workflow was broken down into five sections:

- Dataset Description
- Data Preprocessing
- Building CNN model
- Train and Validate model
- Sign Recognition

The system feeds a continuous video feed into the camera in this manner. The under-lying algorithm extracts features from the incoming image and compares them to a library of traffic signs already in existence. All traffic signals identified by the camera coupled with an algorithm that supports the driver in navigation are displayed on the panel (Fig. 1).

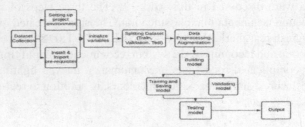

Fig. 1. Flow Diagram

7 Methodology

7.1 Dataset Description

This experiment utilises a Kaggle-provided German Traffic Sign (GTSRB) dataset, which contains approximately 34799 well-structured pixel pictures of signs. Each image in the dataset is assigned to one of 43 classes representing various Traffic Signs. Class 0 = 20 km/h speed limit, class 1 = 30 km/h speed limit, class 2 = 50 km/h speed limit, and so on to class 42 = no passing by vehicles above 3.5 metric tonnes speed restriction. Various traffic sign boards with 43 different signs are included in the set of images. Each of the signs is viewed from a different perspective. Training and testing sets of images are required for model training and validation. As a result, the dataset is partitioned so that 80% of it is used for training, 20% is used for testing, and the remaining 20% is used for validation. That is, the Training set has the shape (22271, 32, 32, 3), the Validation set has the shape (5568, 32, 32, 3), and the Testing set has the shape (5568, 32, 32, 3). (6960, 32, 32, 3) (Fig. 2).

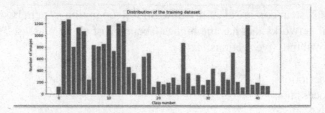

Fig. 2. Dataset Visualization through Plotting

7.2 Data Preprocessing

Pre-processing is a technique in which both the input and output images are intensity images with the least amount of distraction. These images are similar to the sensor's raw data, through an intensity image often signified by a matrix of image function values (Size, Angle, Brightness). The objective of pre-processing is to advance data image by removing undesirable misrepresentations or occasionally enhancing some image features that are significant for further processing. However, geometric transformations of inputs like scaling, rotation, translation are divided as pre-processing methods, and thus parallel methods are used here. In addition, the photos are of varying widths and heights. As a result, all of the photos must be resized to a specific size, such as 32 × 32. After the raw input data has been chosen, one of the most appropriate tasks is to preprocess it. The judgments taken during this stage of development are not suited for a network's performance.

To begin, three pre-processing procedures were applied to data images:

Greyscale- A grayscale image, also known as a gray level image, is one in which the only colours are shades of grey. The reason for this is that there are less features that need to be provided for each pixel in such images than in any other element of a colour image. There is no need to employ more intricate and difficult-to-process colour images because more added grayscale photos are sufficient for image identification. Grayscale is a single layer image with values ranging from 0–255, whereas RGB has three layers. Below is an example of converting a three-channel image to a single grayscale image (Fig. 3).

Fig. 3. Grayscale Images

Image Equalization – If useable data of a picture is given by close variation values, equalization raises the global variation of the image. The intensities can be healthier spread on histogram as a result of this adaptation. This enables places with less local variety to gain more variance. The equalization technique can be implemented using the histogram. Equalization increases the scale range of pixel levels to the whole range in order to improve image variance. Equalization does this by evenly dispersing the most common intensity values. This strategy works well in photographs that have both bright and dark backgrounds and foregrounds.

Image Normalization - Normalization is a technique in image processing that adjusts the range of pixel intensity values by putting mixed images into a similar statistical distribution instead of size and pixel values. The main objective of normalization is to change the values of numeric fields in a database to use a standard range without losing features or changing the ranges of values. Then, remove each image from the dataset mean and divide by its standard deviation to align the image distribution dataset. This makes it easier to simulate training images consistently.

After then, the processed photos were subjected to augmentation.

Data augmentation is a method of extending size of training dataset artificially by creating modified versions of photos in dataset. Augmentation approach can produce contrasts in the images which increase the ability of the fit models to observe what they need to learn to new images. The ImageDataGenerator class in the Keras deep learning neural network toolkit permits to select suitable models with picture data augmentation. Photographs are altered in width, height, zoom, shear, and rotation, resulting in augmented images that are created and saved in the database. The dataset includes photos that aren't directly used. Perhaps the model is given augmented images. Because the augmentations are done at random, it is possible to make customised images as well as close replicas of the original images for use in training.

7.3 Building CNN Model

A convolutional neural network (CNN), a type of artificial neural network used in image recognition and processing. It was created to analyse data in pixels. A CNN employs a concept similar to that of a multilayer perceptron, which was developed to reduce processing time. CNN is made up of several layers, including an input layer, an output layer, and a hidden layer with several convolutional layers, pooling layers, fully connected layers, and normalising layers. Removal of constraints, increase in image processing capability leads a model that is far more operative, similar to trains with partial image processing capability. In simple terms, CNN extracts the image's property and turns it into a lower dimension while preserving its properties.

Because of its excellent accuracy, the developed model employs a Convolutional Neural Network. Four convolutional and two pooling layers make up the CNN. Keras deep learning library was used to create this model. The convolutional layer extracts high-level characteristics from the input image, such as edges and colour gradients. There doesn't have to be just one convolutional layer. It can adjust to high-level features as the number of new layers increases. Pooling layer, like convolutional layer, is used to diminish spatial size of feature. This is done to lower estimation power needed to move on with the data. It can also be used to extract dominating features like rotational and positional invariant. With dimensionality reduction, the max pooling layer removes noisy activation.

Using a fully connected layer to learn the high-level features represented by the output of a convolutional layer is a good technique to do so. The image is then converted into a column vector. Every iteration of training uses backpropagation to feed the flattened output into a neural network. In addition, two dropout layers were added to control the model's overfitting. During training, the dropout layer removes some neurons. The final three layers are fully connected, yielding 43 results computed with the SoftMax activation function. The model is then sorted using the Adam optimizer, which works well and has a loss of "categorical crossentropy" due to the various classes to categorize.

7.4 Train and Validate Model

After built the CNN model architecture, may use model. Fit to train the model (). The accuracy was stable after 20 epochs. The model trained the network with all images in training data set by means of 20 epochs and a batch size of 50. The model was saved as a model trained.h5 file once it was trained. Finally, 99.33% validation accuracy was achieved. The accuracy and loss of training and validation were plotted on a graph (Fig. 4).

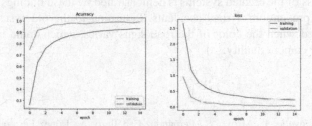

Fig. 4. Validation Results

7.5 Sign Recognition

The proposed system captures the user's image with OpenCV. The names of the signs will be presented from predetermined directories when the model has been trained. If the recognized sign only shows probability if the probability value is larger than the threshold, and the same is true for the other signs. As a result, for each detected sign, the names of the signs are presented.

8 Implementation

(See Fig. 5).

Fig. 5. Implementation Results

9 Conclusion

For traffic sign identification, the proposed system was constructed using Convolutional Neural Network technology, which serves as a Driver Assistance system. The work solution simplifies the end-job user's by taking photographs with a webcam, determining the signs, and displaying the names using a sophisticated and interactive system. With increased accuracy, the system has addressed some of the shortcomings and limits of existing Sign recognition technologies. The model was created with a 99.33% accuracy. The effectiveness of the created systems is demonstrated by these findings. This system will aid in the prevention of road accidents. Returning to the old system, the CNN algorithm is used when the color of the road signs varies, which could be due to bad weather or poor camera quality.

References

1. Bascón, S., Acevedo, J., Arroyo, S., Fernández-Caballero, A., López-Ferreras, F.: An optimization on pictogram identification for the road-sign recognition task using SVMs. Comput. Vis. Image Underst. 114, 373–383 (2010). https://doi.org/10.1016/j.cviu.2009.12.002
2. Ruta, A., Li, Y., Liu, X.: Real-time traffic sign recognition from video by class-specific discriminative features. Pattern Recogn. 43, 416–430 (2010)
3. Broggi, A., Cerri, P., Medici, P., Porta, P.P., Ghisio, G.: Real Time Road Signs Recognition, pp. 981–986 (2007). https://doi.org/10.1109/IVS.2007.4290244
4. Nikam, P.A., Dhaigude, N.B.: A survey on road sign detection and classification. Int. Res. J. Eng. Technol. 04(04) (2017)
5. Keller, C.G., Sprunk, C., Bahlmann, C., Giebel, J., Baratoff, G.: Real-time recognition of U.S. speed signs. IEEE Trans. Intell. Transp. Syst. (2015)
6. Moutarde, F., Bargeton, A., Herbin, A., Chanussot, L.: Robust on-vehicle real-time visual detection of American and European speed limit signs, with a modular traffic signs recognition system. In: 2007 IEEE Intelligent Vehicles Symposium, pp. 1122–1126 (2007). https://doi.org/10.1109/IVS.2007.4290268
7. Radzak, M.Y., Alias, M., Ahmad, M.: Study on Traffic Sign Recognition (2015)
8. Kardkovács, Z., Paróczi, Z., Varga, E., Siegler, A., Lucz, P.: Real-time traffic sign recognition system, pp. 1–5 (2011)
9. Karthikeyan, D., Enitha, C., Bharathi, S., Durkadevi, K.: Traffic sign detection and recognition using image processing. Int. J. Eng. Res. Technol. (IJERT) NCICCT 8(08) (2020)

Assessing Depression Health Information Using Machine Learning

Jebaveerasingh Jebadurai, W. Maria Lebina, and V. Shwetha[✉]

Department of Computer Science, Karunya Institute of Technology and Sciences, Karunya Nagar, Coimbatore, India
jebaveerasingh@karunya.edu, {marialebina, shwetha18}@karunya.edu.in

Abstract. Evaluating health information using machine learning is a must, especially with the tremendous growth of internet resources. Increased usage of technology may result in a less working lifestyle. Furthermore, continual stress on an individual might increase the likelihood of psychosis. Peer pressure, heart attacks, despair, and a variety of other effects are examples of these ailments. Health information should be accurate in most cases People browse the internet before seeing a doctor. Our main idea is the process of evaluating depression treatment guidelines without automation High-precision medical professional intervention. In our idea we used Naive Bayes classifier with high text classification accuracy. In front When using a naive Bayes classifier, treatment guidelines are cleaned up by Stop With words derived from NLTK to avoid meaningless words. Words-in-a-Bag By constructing a recurrence matrix, the technique is utilized to calculate the number of words. The final product is available as a web application.

Keywords: Machine Learning · SVM [Support Vector Machine] · Naïve Bayes classifier · CNN Method

1 Introduction

The most common mental illnesses that people suffer is Depression. Adults and children and ethnicities have already been affected over through the years. Organizational climate, endorphin activities, mental instabilities, relationship problems, and social interactions all increase the risk of depression. Machine learning is a type of intelligence application (AI) Give the system the capacity to learn and develop on its own from experience that isn't evident in the software. The practice of assigning tags or categories to text based on its content is known as text categorization. This is a fundamental job in natural language processing (NLP) that has a wide range of applications [1]. According to the CDC, between 2013 and 2016, 10.4% of girls were diagnosed with depression, compared to 5.5% of men. WHO estimates that depression affects more than 300 million people worldwide? It is also the number one reason for disability around the world. The main causes of suicide and A global disorder is depression. If left untreated, [2] it can affect the daily life of those around the patient. Depression in the family, work, or society depression. It causes negative thoughts, reduces, reduces concentration on work. Performance. It also affects the human reproductive system existence. Evidence-based medicine is promoted in the medical field. The original model was published in the Journal of the American Medical Association. Weight gain/loss, heart disease, inflammation, sexual health problems, chronic health problems, sleep disorders, gastric problems, and other major symptoms and effects include changes in food and sleep habits, loss of energy, lack of concentration, anxiety, hopelessness, feeling of less use, taught of self-harming, and other major symptoms and effects include weight gain/loss, heart disease, inflammation, sexual health problems, chronic health problems, sleep disorders, gastric problems, and so on [3]. According to "322 million people worldwide suffer from depression," according to global data. In 2002, the World Health Organization (WHO) has classified unipolar depression as a handicap, predicting that it would be the second biggest cause by 2030 [9]. In 2017, the WHO launched the "Let's Talk" campaign to promote awareness about the significance of talking about it.

2　Literature Survey

The work that is relevant to this inquiry is examined in depth. For example, is a variable input in all investigations, Text and Comment on Wed application [1]. For testing part school students square measure asked totally different questionnaires and videos of scholar's square measure collected whereas detection of options throughout the Wed application, the facial options of those student's square measure extracted and normalized. For the take a look at dataset then the extraction of countenance depression detection. Within the coaching part the ecstatic, contempt, and disgust choices derived from of the source positive vibe dataset are used to train the SVM classifier. The alternatives collected from just about every picture of the datasets collected are checked using this trained SVM to see if they are correct. Options depression is obtained from the extent of those options. It's been seen that depression and different mental diseases might cause people to use social media to precise their joy.

[1]　Successively number all equations. Numbers in equations, inside You may use to make your equations more compact by using Instead of 3, use a long dash. The Bayes Theorem is an important part of the probability and statistics world. It denotes a foreseeing atmosphere. Several ecstatic, anger, and disgusted choices derived from either the source positive vibe datasets are used to train the Support vector Machine (SVM). All variables collected on every picture of the datasets collected are checked and used this trained SVM to see if they are correct.

[2]　In speech, feature engineering entails extracting features frame by frame, computing statistical measures, characteristics. Characteristics include fused and Principal Component Analysis are the statistical methods done on the features retrieved. Because there are fewer sad people available, there may be an imbalance. The data set is divided between 60% training and 40% testing. The merged context information from the training program is used to train Vector Support Machine (SVM) networks, but the data source yielded spurious regression. Anxiety identification classification models are change functions that translate data into higher dimensions in order to locate a higher dimensional space that can class the material,

which category may not be possible in the original data. The fresh data that the classifier is supplied with is also resulted in a rise dimension. Linear and SVM are performed first, followed by the kernel. The assessment measures for each classifier are constructed sequentially across the DIACWOZ data corpus. Using acoustic parameters, a Classification Model (DCM)" is developed with a 93% accuracy on validation data set. (PCA) is used to minimize the size of the feature space.

[3] Depression Prediction Victimization is created as a model. RapidMiner The model is made up of a number of processes that are used to verify each other. It has two datasets and seven major operators. The first dataset is the coaching dataset, which comprises the manually just in case of depressed sentiment), and the trained post is in the third column. Tokenize operations divide a document's text into a filter. Stop-words removes each token from a document, filtering out English stop-words. This applies to the coaching dataset, which is divided into two sections: training and testing.

[4] NLP and ML methodologies are also used to start creating (or 'train') 'classification techniques' that categorize health records based on their contents. These health-related classifiers are either reliable or not after being trained based on a set of criteria. Textual characteristics were retrieved that define important elements of health information quality. Going to follow that, machine learning algorithms were used to understand from those kinds of attributes in order to identify specific health data and achieve the ultimate goal of providing trustworthy mental wellbeing information so that individuals may make an educated decision around individual medical needs. This research heavily relied on machine learning libraries. In this post, we will look at how machine learning algorithms learn to categorize unseen documents into the appropriate class based on the extracted characteristics from them. Word n-grams, punctuation marks, word, sentence, and document length are all text-based characteristics that are widely utilized in this type of analysis. Some of the domain-specific criteria utilized as characteristics were taken from the four JAMA criteria (if a document meets these criteria).

3 Methodology

This System determine the web content of despair remedy fitness information routinely with the assist of supervised system learning strategies. In this gadget, it is straightforward to validate whether the content material is legitimate or not via computerized evaluation method. Moreover, it is straightforward for those who mixture health web sites as maximum of the phases of validation is finished manually, while this gadget does the identical thing manually. The first step in this system is to collect the appropriate dataset corpus. Once The dataset will be collected. Must be placed in the required file format The conversion will take place. The placed record is passed to the next stage as input. Then the dataset is pre-processed. H. Dataset needs to be cleaned up in advance It is supplied to the machine. In this system, records are filled with text analysis and text mining. First, the machine wishes to be dropped often words that appear from textual facts or common phrases [5] or very small meanings like comparable phrases inclusive of "and", "or" "that". This is done to enhance machine performance. Stemming after getting rid of the stop word the stop. Stemming is a strategy for removing affixes from a word and ending up at the root. Cook, for example, is the origin of the word. Instead of keeping all words, the system simply saves stem words, considerably lowering index size while enhancing index performance. Retrieval precision Giving the cleaned text set as input to the classifier model is the next step. This In basic terms, this section will transform the text collection into a machine comprehensible format. To put it another way, it translates text to binary numbers (0s and 1s). The classifier's output in a 75:25 ratio, the model is split into training and test sets. After splitting, the training data is sent into the naive Bayes classifier, and the system trains the data [13]. On the other hand, the test data is fed into the trained machine to see if the system works properly with the classifier. The last step is to deploy the preceding phases as a single web application by integrating the machine learning code with the HTML and JavaScript using the Python Flask environment. The dataset used in this article is from Kaggle. It has a unique entry for 10283 and has two parameters: message and label. Message parameters consist of pressed and non-pressed text. The digits 0 and 1 make up the Caption element. Non-repressive content is symbolized by "0," whereas suppressive text is symbolized by "1." (Fig. 1).

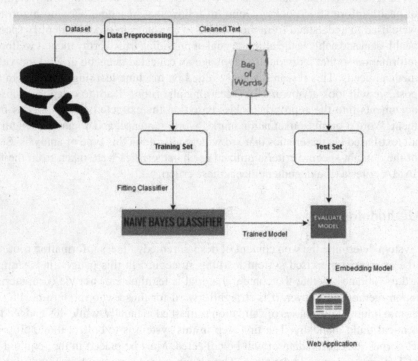

Fig. 1. Block Diagram

3.1 Data Pre-processing

The first and most important step in evaluating health websites in machine learning is to undertake data preparation. Pre-processing refers to the adjustments we apply to our data before feeding it to the algorithm. Data Pre-processing is a method for transforming unclean data into a utilizable dataset. In other words, anytime data is collected from several sources, it is the data was obtained in raw format, which made analysis impossible. The text components in the dataset must be appropriately formatted to generate better results from the applied model in Machine Learning projects. Some Machine Learning models require data in a specific format; for example, the Random Forest algorithm does not support null values; as a result, null values from the original raw dataset must be handled before the Random Forest algorithm can be applied. Data scraped from the web often contains HTML entities such as <, >, &, which are contained in the source data. As a result, these entities must be removed in order for the algorithms to produce accurate results without text errors when classifying their class [10]. The unwanted entities can be directly removed using specific regular expressions. As the dataset contains enormous data, the machine needs to speed up the cleaning process in order to achieve the result. Stop-words (frequently occurring words) should be eliminated. One can either make a big list of stop-words or use language-specific libraries which have already been created. Human expressions such as [laughing], [crying], and [audience paused] can be found in textual data (typically speech transcripts). These expressions are occasionally irrelevant to the context of the speech and should be eliminated as a result [5]. Within the code below if exploit 25% of the info for testing and the remainder of the 75% for coaching. There's an easy workaround for this mistreatment the "sklearn" command to indiscriminately choose sure index numbers then use the chosen index numbers to split the dataset into two parts: a training set and a testing set.

3.2 The Bag-of-Words Model

The optimization technique, popularly known as the bag-of-words method, seems to be a simplified model used within language processing and retrieval (IR). This paradigm represents a sentence (other than a phrase or a paper) as a bag (multiset) among its words, that also ignores grammar and perhaps even vocabulary items while keeping multiplicity. The bag-of-words notion has also been used in computer vision. The bag of words model is commonly employed in message different classifiers that use the (percent of) frequency of each word to build a classification model. The count of each word is then represented using vectors. The number of times each word appears in the corpus is recorded by each element (text sample). Some words in the English language are exceedingly frequent, such as "is," "the," and "a." If we examine their raw frequency, we may or may not be able to understand the difference between different categories of documents. A frequent solution is to employ a statistical approach known as frequency-inverse document frequency (tf-idf).

3.3 Naïve Bayes Algorithm

It is already a classification level approach that is based on the Bayesian network and hence the arrogant assumption of predictive self-rule. In simple terms, a Naïve mathematical classifier holds that the availability of one feature in a given system is indicative of the presence of another feature. For example, if a vegetable is red, spherical, and about 3 inches in diameter, it is referred to as AN apple. Although these traits are squarely reliant on each other or on the existence of other features, they all increase the likelihood how this fruit is an apple, which is why it is referred to be Naïve Bayes [2] The Bayes Theorem is a fundamental concept in statistics and probability. It expresses the probability of an event occurring based on factors that the user is aware of ahead of time [15]. The Bayesian algorithm is one of the most often used techniques in the Machine Learning environment due to its simplicity, efficiency, and usage in the predictive context. Its foundation is Bayesian' Theorem.

The Bayesian algorithm must be used to compute the posterior distribution P(A|B) given P(A), P(B), and P(A|B). Refer to the following equation:

$$P(A|B) = \frac{P(B|A) \cdot P(A)}{P(B)} \tag{1}$$

- P(A|B) is the posterior probability of class (a, target) given predictor (b, attribute's)
- P(B|A) is the likelihood which is the probability of predictor given class.
- P(A) is the prior probability of class.
- P(B) is the prior probability of predictor.

The [6] Naïve Bayesian classifier's decision-making task is to assess whether the presented input is correct or incorrect. The Naïve Bayesian Model was trained using the training data set, which is then used to predict the output. The classifier determines the output by computing the Posterior Probability. The test set is predicted using a naive Bayes classifier trained set [12]. Naïve Bayes is a simple and fast method for predicting inside a given data frame, with the potential to predict several classes. When assumptions are taken into consideration, the Nave Bayes method performs better than other algorithms and requires less training data. The Naïve Bayes method, although, has certain limitations. If any classification model is absent while predicting in any category, a zero is assigned, making further prediction impossible. This is known as "Zero Frequency," and the Naïve Bayes algorithm's predictions is not 100% correct.

3.4 Simple CNN Classifier Model

Massive volumes of classification model may be required for supervised learning with (CNNs). CNNs are a type of deep neural network that uses the notion of local receptive fields and weight replication to create a new type of network [1]. CNNs consist of a combination of convolutional and subsampling layers that help extract meaningful representations of the input data. The above design comprises a single convolution operation, which is followed by a fully linked layer towards the maximum overtime pooling layer. The convolution layer receives a matrix as input, with each row being a vector representation of a word in the treatment guideline and uses various filters to identify local characteristics [11]. Each filter's output is passed into a pooling layer, which looks for the highest value. To acquire the feature representation of input, the output feature maps corresponding to the filters utilized are eventually concatenated. The probability distribution across the two classes, as well as the loss function, are calculated in the last layer.

3.5 Support Vector Machine

Because of its simplicity, the SVM method outperforms all other algorithms in terms of usability. All of the data is treated as a point (a dot) on a graph with a dimension of 'n' space in this method. We define dimensions of 'n' space as the number of attributes or data points that must be represented in sequence to be referred to be a characteristic in the graph [2]. The hyper-plane is used in SVM to separate two classes in dimension 'n' space, and the emphasis is utilized to find the hyper-plane. There are numerous different hyperplanes, but even the main purpose is to select one with the shortest distance between the data components exhibited spots of the 2 classes. Every number of parameters determines the percentage of [14] the hyperplane produced; for ex, if there are two main parameters, the hyperplane is one dimensional (a line), and if there are three attributes, the hyperplane is two dimensional (a triangle) (though it becomes more complicated if the number of features exceeds each of) [3]. The hyperplane's location and orientation are greatly aided by support vectors. They're the spots on the data components that are near to the hyperplane. The classifier's margin is increased to its maximum with these vectors. This same algorithm generates linear output; if the output is 1, it is regarded as one class; if the output is -1, it is recognized as a distinct class, resulting in the SVM margins range of $[-1, 1]$.

$$c(x, y, f(x)) = \{ \begin{matrix} 0, & \text{if } y * f(x) \geq 1 \\ 1 - y * f(x), & else \end{matrix} \tag{2}$$

The categorization is carried out in order to separate the data into categories. The minimum number of courses is necessary [2]. The number of training samples in this case is, The SVM uses an optimum hyperplane to partition the data into two categories: depressed and non-depressed. This will classify the data supplied into two groups: [7] Whether you're depressed or not is a personal choice. The network is provided along with a variety of social media platforms of various types, and indeed, the network is built to categorize those into the two major categories indicated.

3.6 Random Forest Algorithm

Random Forest is a supervised learning system that uses a huge number of decision trees to construct a network. For classification and regression, it employs an ensemble learning technique [3]. A decision tree is a tool that allows you to make decisions based on the results of each stage. The architecture of decision trees is similar to that of flow diagrams. Trees contain three crucial components: nodes (root and leaf), branches, and leaves, and decision trees have the same. ([2] In a random forest, the data for every decision tree is chosen at random. To put it another way, each tree creates a random set of data. As a result, we have uncorrelated decision trees [8]. The inaccuracy created by a single tree is nullified by the combined effect of several uncorrelated trees. Random forest is a clustering algorithm for generating prediction model that involves training a large number of decision trees and then returning the mode of the individual decision trees classes. Throughout the RF model, they applied Gini as a criterion and 10 parameter estimation.

4   Experimental Analysis and Result

On the three aforementioned datasets, several experiments were conducted using various classifiers trained on various combinations of characteristics. Since this samples are just so short, still about 15% of the total from every corpus was maintained as test data. The majority of the samples (85%) are often used as training phase. The following machine learning classification methods worked well: Gaussian Naive Bayes had an accuracy of 84%, Random Forest had a 56% accuracy, Support Vector Machine (SVM) had a 68% accuracy, Simple CNN and BOW from the spacy module had a 94% accuracy. After applying the above algorithm, Simple CNN turns out to be better at predicting depression-related sentences with 97% accuracy compared to the four algorithms. This is because Simple CNN is the model under the scrapy module, which is primarily used for analyzing text-based data. Gaussian Naive Bayes worked well with 84% accuracy (Table 1).

Table 1. Accuracies obtained from various Machine Learning algorithms

Algorithm Used	Accuracy
Naïve Bayes Algorithm	0.84
Simple CNN Classifier Model	0.97
Support Vector Machine	0.68
Random Forest Algorithm	0.56
The Bag of Word	0.94

5   Conclusion

Because the bulk of humans are searching for fitness statistics via fitness websites, the accuracy of fitness statistics is critical. Incorrect statistics must be avoided. Using device gaining knowledge of approaches, the recommended version routinely analyses despair remedy statistics and completes the assessment manner fast. It additionally ensures that statistics approximately despair remedy is accurate.

Acknowledgement. The authors acknowledge the computational facilities provided by Karunya Institute of Technology and Sciences through the CISCO Center of Excellence for Advanced Networking in the Department of Computer Science and Engineering.

References

1. Narayanrao, P.V., Kumari, P.L.S.: Analysis of machine learning algorithms for predicting depression. In: 2020 International Conference on Computer Science, Engineering and Applications (ICCSEA), pp. 1–4. IEEE (2020)
2. Geetha, G., Saranya, G., Chakrapani, K., Ponsam, J.G., Safa, M., Karpagaselvi, S.: Early detection of depression from social media data using machine learning algorithms. In: 2020 International Conference on Power, Energy, Control and Transmission Systems (ICPECTS), pp. 1–6. IEEE (2020)
3. Yalamanchili, B., Kota, N.S., Abbaraju, M.S., Nadella, V.S.S., Alluri, S.V.: Real-time acoustic based depression detection using machine learning techniques. In: International Conference on Emerging Trends in Information Technology and Engineering (ic-ETITE) 2020, pp. 1–6. IEEE (2020)
4. Aldarwish, M.M., Ahmad, H.F.: Predicting depression levels using social media posts. In: IEEE 13th International Symposium on Autonomous Decentralized System (ISADS) 2017, pp. 277–280. IEEE (2017)
5. Al-Jefri, M.M., Evans, R., Ghezzi, P., Uchyigit, G.: Using machine learning for automatic identification of evidence-based health information on the web, In: International Conference on Digital Health 2017, pp. 167–174 (2017)
6. Sau, A., Bhakta, I.: Predicting anxiety and depression in elderly patients using machine learning technology. Healthc. Technol. Lett. **4**(6), 238–243 (2017)
7. Sah, R.D., Sheetlani, J., Kumar, D.R., Sahu, I.N.: Migraine (headaches) disease data classification using data mining classifiers. Quest J. Res. Environ. Earth Sci. **3**, 10–16 (2017)
8. Pineda, A.L., Ye, Y., Visweswaran, S., Cooper, G.F., Wagner, M.M., Tsui, F.R.: Comparison of machine learning classifiers for influenza detection from emergency department free-text reports. J. Biomed. Inform. **58**, 60–69 (2015)
9. Alghamdi, N.S.: Monitoring mental health using smart devices with text analytical tool. In: 2019 6th International Conference on Control, Decision and Information Technologies (CoDIT), pp. 2046–2051. IEEE (2019)
10. Chen, T., Su, P., Shang, C., Hill, R., Zhang, H., Shen, Q.: Sentiment classification of drug reviews using fuzzy-rough feature selection. In: IEEE International Conference on Fuzzy Systems (FUZZ-IEEE) 2019, pp. 1–6. IEEE (2019)
11. Ahmed, A., Sultana, R., Ullas, Md.T.R., Begom, M., Rahi, Md.M.I., Alam, Md.A.: A machine learning approach to detect depression and anxiety using supervised learning. In: IEEE Asia-Pacific Conference on Computer Science and Data Engineering (CSDE) 2020, pp. 1–6. IEEE (2020)
12. Joseph, R., Udupa, S., Jangale, S., Kotkar, K., Pawar, P.: Employee attrition using machine learning and depression analysis. In: 5th International Conference on Intelligent Computing and Control Systems (ICICCS) 2021, pp. 1000–1005. IEEE (2021)
13. Ding, Y., Chen, X., Fu, Q., Zhong, S.: A depression recognition method for college students using deep integrated support vector algorithm. IEEE Access **8**, 75616–75629 (2020)
14. Khalil, R.M., Al-Jumaily, A.: Machine learning based prediction of depression among type 2 diabetic patients. In: 12th International Conference on Intelligent Systems and Knowledge Engineering (ISKE) 2017, pp. 1–5. IEEE (2017)
15. Kamite, S.R., Kamble, V.B.: Detection of depression in social media via twitter using machine learning approach. In: International Conference on Smart Innovations in Design, Environment, Management, Planning and Computing (ICSIDEMPC) 2020, pp. 122–125. IEEE (2020)

An Optimal and Authentic Communication System Based on Authorization Card Repudiation to Perform a Secure Data Communication in MANET

J. Anitha Josephine[1], S. Senthilkumar[2]([✉]), R. Rajkumar[3] [iD],
and C. M. Arun Kumar[4] [iD]

[1] Department of AIML, School of Engineering, Malla Reddy University, Hyderabad, India
[2] Department of CSE, University College of Engineering, Pattukkottai, India
senthilucepkt@gmail.com
[3] DSBS, SRM Institute of Science and Technology, Kattankulathur, India
[4] Department of ECE, University College of Engineering, Pattukkottai, India

Abstract. Due to easiness in implementation and mobility, Mobile adhoc networks (MANETs) are focused as a major communication environment in the current scenario. The major challenge to any MANET environment is based on security treats given by the malevolent and illegal processing. To address these challenges, this research paper proposes an optimal cluster based authorization card repudiation technique to provide a secure data communication in MANET against the malevolent activities and illegal process. The proposed architecture describes the structure of the environment as cluster development, selecting the cluster chief, authorization card administrator, node classification, card repudiation and verification of incorrect allegation. The PLMS clustering algorithm is expanded as P stands for power, L stands for link, M stands for move ble and S stands for signal to noise ratio. The following parameters such as victorious card ratio (VCR), resolving time (RT), average card delay (ACD), Packet delivery ratio (PDR), and overall throughput of the environment are considered to justify the performance of the proposed system. As a result, when comparing to other existing systems, the proposed system provides optimal and secure communication in the MANET.

Keywords: MANET · Card repudiation · Security · Power · Link · Moveable · Signal to noise ratio

1 Introduction

The arbitrary topology is formed through the wireless links in which the collection of mobile routers has the connection with the MANET. At present, different types of applications such as VANET based wireless communication, observing the health systems, mobile networking and emergency alert system [1, 2]. As per the demand, the MANETs

R. Venkataraman et al. (Eds.): ICIoT 2022, CCIS 1727, pp. 54–64, 2023.
https://doi.org/10.1007/978-3-031-28475-5_6

mobile node which have a random movement combines with other nodes in the environment. There is no structured infrastructure for MANETs regarding to the mobile communication. Due to this, there may be a chance of security issues such as processing of malevolent activities and illegal user entry in the network whereas these types of attacks are very difficult to identify in the network [3]. The existing system named TAEACK was proposed to identify and eliminate the illegal nodes and malevolent activities from the environment [4]. A valid acknowledgement should be passed among the communication nodes to ensure the security in the MANET. The acknowledgement is done based on the authorization card. Without issuing the authorization card, the communication among the nodes in MANET will not take place [5]. The authorization card methodology recognizing the malevolent node with the help of faith authorization from other already present node in the network [6]. Mostly, when the malevolent node is identified, it should be discarded or stopped from the network with minimum networks overhead. In common, MANETs contains the characters such as minimum infrastructures, non-static topology, immediateness, distributed routing methodology. At the time of attacking, the hacker will not modify the exchanged data [7]. The attackers won't consider the integrity or confidentiality while tracking the data in the network. In common, process of the network won't be affected by the passive attack. In authorization card repudiation based security technique in MANETs it is very difficult to identify the passive attacks in the network. To solve these problems in MANET many existing systems provided the solution [8]. An important solution is to use techniques based on encryption to encrypt the exchanged information among the nodes. The malevolent user or illegal user affect the network through the process of active attacks. In MANET, the information exchanged between the sender and receiver can be altered by the malevolent node or illegal user through the active attack. The active attacks can be either occur inside and outside of the network. The agreement nodes process the inside active attacks whereas the external attacks are established by the mobile nodes in which these mobile nodes are not part of the mobile network. An important issue is that identifying the inside active attacks whereas most of the dependent nodes are part of the mobile environment.

2 Literature Review

The various security issues faced by the MANETs are solved using many existing security methods [9–14]. The chances are more for the malevolent users or illegal users to attack the MANET, because the MANET doesn't have any valid structure based on mobile communication. It is very important to discard the attacker node from the overall environment instead of just identifying the attacker node and separating the node from the network. This is to done to ensure the non-occurrence of the illegal node or malevolent node in the network which can perform operation malevolent activities inside the network. In this regard, the solution should be given by discarding the malevolent or illegal node from the entire network [15]. Security based on trust and security based on authentication are the two major security types available in the MANET. In our research work security based on authentication has been concentrated in which it suits for the proposed cluster based authorization repudiation. The important problem for the routing optimization in MANETs are the environment which falls under the shortage of basic management, non-static process, condition based resource restrictions. One of the important solution for the bisecting the network into same type of groups will be performing the clustering among the nodes based on their similarities. For such situation, one of the node in the cluster will be selected as a chief cluster of the network. The cluster chief's primary responsibility is to establish local coordination operations while also establishing internal and external communication channels that are based on the cluster and cluster management [16]. The existing system with the ability of vindicate was used one of the security technique based on the authorization card repudiation for the MANET which evaluated the parameters accuracy and repudiation time. The disadvantage of the existing was; it allows many security attacks in the environment [17]. The clustering for secure communication was used to provide high security to the MANET but it also allows many security attacks this is major disadvantage of the system which evaluates the parameters such as mobility, faith value, stability and connectivity [18].

The key management and encryption was used to increase the performance metrics of the MANET using the algorithm called key management with authentication which evaluates the management cost, average delay and packet delivery cost. The major disadvantage of the system is maximum end to end delay [19]. Another clustering based protocol to provide the security for the MANET to ensure that the malevolent nodes will generate the false authorization card among the nodes in the network. The parameters evaluated are failure and successful rate. The major disadvantage was unpredictable destination rate [20]. Threshold based cluster signature was another existing system which enables the privacy protection methodology for trusted entity in the network. The parameters evaluated are security, performance and correctness.

3 Proposed Method

In this study, a cluster-based authorization card repudiation algorithm is used to find out the malevolent node in the MANET. The security issues in MANET are solved by using the proposed approach. In this research paper, the algorithm called PLMS clustering algorithm has been proposed to develop the clusters and to detect the cluster chief in each and every cluster. The PLMS clustering algorithm is expanded as P stands for power, L stands for link, M stands for moveable and S stands for signal to noise ratio.

3.1 Residue or Balance Power

In general, all the cluster chiefs (CC) should manage maximum residual power while comparing with the already occurred node in the network. The deviation between the initial power and utilized power is used to identify the available power. The residual power of a node at a given point in time t, P(t) is calculated by

$$P(t) = (T_{np} * c) + (R_{np} * d) \qquad (1)$$

where, T_{np} is the total no of transmitted data packets.

R_{np} is the total no of received data packets

c, d represents the constants of the range 0 & 1

In common, residue power (P) = Initial Power (IP) – Utilized power (UP), the total residue power Pres at time t is defined by

$$P_{res} = P_i - P(t) \tag{2}$$

3.2 Link

The link is detected based on the number of nodes that are already present for the destination nodes. The link concept is divided into types such as communication inside the cluster and communication outside the cluster. In the type, communication inside the cluster, the nodes available in the network passes it described data to the cluster chief. Whereas, communication outside the cluster, each and every cluster chiefs transfers the collected data to their nearest cluster chiefs.

3.3 Anticipated Corresponding Moveable (ACM)

The movability of the node is described based on the moveable speed and direction. The corresponding moveable of the server Sj at immediate time t is described as

$$CM^t_{(i,j)} = \sqrt[2]{(sp^t_i)^2 + (sp^t_j)^2 - [2sp^t_i sp^t_j \cos(\theta^t_i - \theta^t_j)]} \tag{3}$$

The ACM is estimated between two server's S_i and S_j as

$$ACM^t_{(i,j)} = \frac{1}{st} \sum_{t-1}^{st} CM^t_{(i,j)} \tag{4}$$

where, sp^t_j depicts the speed of the server node S_j, θ^t_j depicts the corresponding moveable direction of the server node S_j, and t depicts the time and t shows the number of stages.

3.4 Signal to Noise Ratio

The signal to noise ratio (SNR) depicts the stage of a prescribed signal to the stage of noise based on contextual.

The estimation of the signal to noise ratio (SNR) depends on the below mathematical term as

$$SNR = 10 \log_{10}\left(\frac{HF^2}{mean\ square\ error}\right) \tag{5}$$

where, HF depicts the high fluctuation among the nodes. These four components power (p), link (L), Moveable (M) and signal to noise ratio (SNR) are joined as a collection to calculate the node weight. The node weight NW is described by,

$$NW = nw_1 * P + nw_2 * L + nw_3 * M + nw_4 * SNR \tag{6}$$

For the range between 0 and 1, the values of nw1, nw2, nw3 and nw4 may differ.

$$nw_1 + nw_2 + nw_3 + nw_4 = 1 \tag{7}$$

In this research, these node weights are used to identify cluster chiefs.

3.5 Cluster Chief Selection

Each node's estimated weight is compared to the weights of all other nodes in the cluster. Based on the weights, one of the best nodes is chosen to be the cluster chief. The procedure for choosing the cluster chief is outlined below.

3.5.1 Algorithm 1: Authorization Card Repudiation

Step 1: **Begin** the procedure, identify the nearest nodes for each and every nodes and update in the nearest node database

Step 2: The Node weight NW has been calculated for each and every node based on the power (p), link (L), Moveable (M) and signal to noise ratio (SNR) as specified in the equation 6.

Step 3: Each and every node has to publish its node weight NW value to its nearest nodes.

Step 4: **if** (node weight NW of node B is greater than (>) node weights of all the nearest nodes)

    {
    Then Node B is elected as the chief cluster
    }

Step 5: The Node B publishes the chief cluster details to all other nodes which are present already in the environment.

Step 6: **End** the procedure.

3.6 Steps Involved in the Authorization Card Repudiation

In the procedure of authorization card repudiation, the nodes which are all occurred in the environment is observed through the one bound nearest nodes. The one of the objective of these nearest nodes are to identify and collect the malevolent data about the sensor nodes present in the environment.

3.6.1   Algorithm2: Authorization Card Repudiation

Step 1: Identify the malevolent operation of node n by nearest nodes m_i ($i = 1,2, , , ,$
m) and throws an allegation packet against the node n.
Step 2: Publish the allegation packet to the gateway GW
Step 3: Load the allegations in the pending record of GW gateway and check the
allegations based on its time of arrival (TA).
Step 4: if (pending record = empty)
      {
               Proceed to last step
}
     else
     {
     GW gateway checks the initial arrived allegation provided by node 'Y'
}
Step 5: GW gateway updates A_y and A_n
$ A_y = total count of allegations produced by node 'i'
$ A_n = total count of allegations produced against node 'i'
Step 6: Identify the allegations weight of node y and n
$$WT_y = 1 - \lambda\,(arrival)a_y - \lambda(arrival)A_y$$
Step 7: if ($WT_y > WT_n$)
  {
               Proceed to step 8
  }
  else
  {
               Again perform step 4 to step 7
  }
Step 8: The pending record (PR) is completed by the gateway GR and malevolent
node 'n' is included to the ACRR; publishing the repudiation details to the network; A_y
is updated as minus one for each and every proved allegation node 'n'.

Step 9: Each and every node in the network environment updates its local ACRR
based on the received repudiation data.

The common nodes verify the authorization card repudiation Record (ACRR)
whether the nearest node occurred in the ACRR. The procedure is given in the flowchart
of Fig. 1.

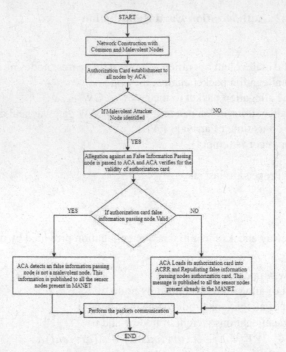

Fig. 1. Working of the Authorization card repudiation procedure

4   Results and Discussions

This research work depicts the outcome evaluation of the suggested cluster-based authorization card repudiation method based on the different parameters such as victorious card ratio (VCR), resolving time (RT), average card delay (ACD), Packet delivery ratio (PDR), delay based on end -end communication and the overall throughput of the environment.

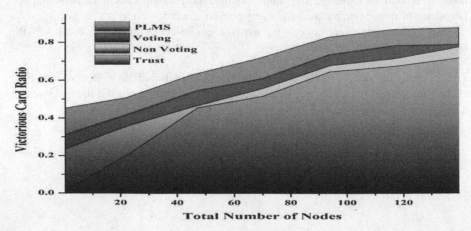

Fig. 2. Victorious Card Ratio

The VCR is determined as the ratio of the number of victorious card operations to the sum of the requests for such operations. The comparison and performance graph is shown in the Fig. 2. Resolving Time depicts the time required for every nodes in the environment to establish the legitimate authorization card. The comparison and performance graph is shown in the Fig. 3. The ACD is quantitatively evaluated and performance graph is shown in the Fig. 4.

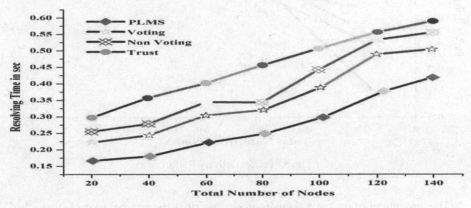

Fig. 3. Resolving Time (RT)

The packet delivery ratio is measured as the ratio of sum of number of packets transferred and sum of number of packets reached the destination without any problem. The comparison and performance graph of packet delivery ratio is shown in the Fig. 5

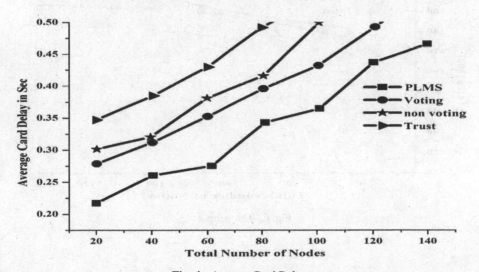

Fig. 4. Average Card Delay.

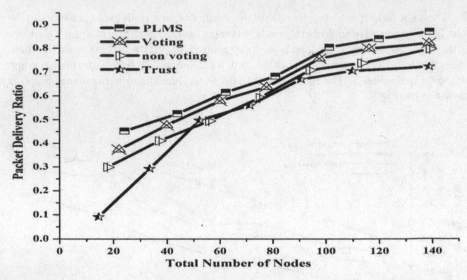

Fig. 5. Packet Delivery Ratio.

The throughput of the overall environment describes the number of packets reached the destination without any problem for the particular time. The comparison and performance graph based on throughput is shown in the Fig. 6.

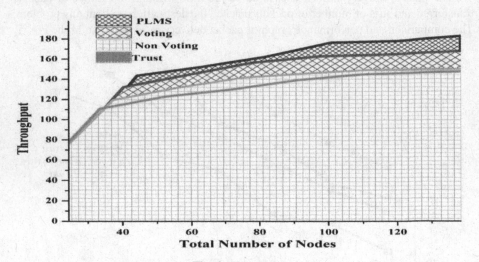

Fig. 6. Throughput.

5   Conclusions

Our research work proposed PLMS cluster based authorization card repudiation methodology to handle the security problems in MANETs. The objective of the proposed model is used to separate the malevolent nodes and protecting the network from these malevolent node operations. The PLMS proposed algorithm elects the optimal cluster chief in each cluster. The repudiation node evaluates the authorization card based on the authorization card repudiation procedure. The combination of voting and non-voting algorithm is used to repudiate the authorization card of the malevolent nodes and clears the illegal allegations or false allegations on the legal nodes.

The parameters such as victorious card ratio (VCR), resolving time (RT), average card delay (ACD), Packet delivery ratio (PDR), and overall throughput of the environment are considered to justify the performance of the proposed system. In the future, it is planned to enhance the proposed algorithm to maximize the data communication by solving the security issues in an effective manner.

References

1. Giridhar, R., Suresh, S.: Cluster based certificate authority scheme in WSN. In: International Conference on Wireless Communications, Signal Processing and Networking (WiSPNET), pp. 367–371. IEEE (2016)
2. Patil, B., Biradar, S.R.: Cluster based authentication scheme for wireless multimedia sensor networks. In: Proceedings of the Second International Conference on Information and Communication Technology for Competitive Strategies, p. 99. ACM (2016)
3. Gañán, C., Muñoz, J.L., Esparza, O., Mata-Díaz, J., Alins, J.: PPREM: privacy preserving revocation mechanism for vehicular ad hoc networks. Comput. Stand. Interfaces **36**(3), 513–523 (2014)
4. Venkata Swaroop, G., Murugaboopathi, G., Kalaiselvan, S.A.: TAEACK: a time adaptive enhanced ACK mechanism for detecting and preventing sink-hole attacks in MANET. Aust. J. Basic Appl. Sci. **9**(27), 291–299 (2015)
5. Raya, M., Papadimitratos, P., Hubaux, J.P.: Securing vehicular communications. IEEE Wirel. Commun. **13**(5), 8–15 (2006)
6. Rabieh, K., Mahmoud, M., Tonyali, S.: Scalable certificate revocation schemes for smart grid AMI networks using bloom filters. IEEE Trans. Dependable Secure Comput. **14**(4), 420–432 (2017)
7. Azer, M.A., El-Kassas, S.M., El-Soudani, M.S.: Certification and revocation schemes in ad hoc networks survey and challenges. In: ICSNC 2007, Second International Conference on Systems and Networks Communications, p. 17. IEEE (2007)
8. Thein, M.C.M., Thein, T.: An energy efficient cluster-head selection for wireless sensor networks. In: 2010 International Conference on Intelligent Systems, Modelling and Simulation (ISMS), pp. 287–291. IEEE (2010)
9. Varatharajan, R., Manogaran, G., Priyan, M.K., Sundarasekar, R.: Wearable sensor devices or early detection of Alzheimer disease using dynamic time warping algorithm. Clust. Comput. (2017). https://doi.org/10.1007/s10586-017-0977-2
10. Varatharajan, R., Manogaran, G., Priyan, M.K., Balaş, V.E., Barna, C.: Visual analysis of geospatial habitat suitability model based on inverse distance weighting with paired comparison analysis. Multimed. Tools Appl. **77**(14), 17573–17593 (2017). https://doi.org/10.1007/s11042-017-4768-9

11. Varatharajan, R., Vasanth, K., Gunasekaran, M., Priyan, M., Gao, X.Z.: An adaptive decision based kriging interpolation algorithm for the removal of high density salt and pepper noise in images. Comput. Electr. Eng. (2017). https://doi.org/10.1016/j.compeleceng.2017.05.035Get

12. Rabieh, K., Mahmoud, M.M., Akkaya, K., Tonyali, S.: Scalable certificate revocation schemes for smart grid AMI networks using bloom filters. IEEE Trans. Dependable Secure Comput. **14**(4), 420–432 (2017)

13. Khan, T., et al.: Certificate revocation in vehicular ad hoc networks techniques and protocols: a survey. Sci. China Inf. Sci. **60**(10), 100301 (2017)

14. Raja, J.B., Pandian, S.C., Pamina, J.: Certificate revocation mechanism in mobile ADHOC grid architecture. Int. J. Comput. Sci. Trends Technol. **5**, 125–130 (2017)

15. Singh, B., Lobiyal, D.K.: A novel energy-aware cluster head selection based on particle swarm optimization for wireless sensor networks. Hum. Centric Comput. Inf. Sci. **2**(1), 13 (2012)

16. Kang, S.H., Nguyen, T.: Distance based thresholds for cluster head selection in wireless sensor networks. IEEE Commun. Lett. **16**(9), 1396–1399 (2012)

17. Liu, W., Nishiyama, H., Ansari, N., Yang, J., Kato, N.: Cluster based certificate revocation with vindication capability for mobile ad hoc networks. IEEE Trans. Parallel Distrib. Syst. **24**(2), 239–249 (2013)

18. Rachedi, A., Benslimane, A.: A secure architecture for mobile Ad Hoc networks. In: Cao, J., Stojmenovic, I., Jia, X., Das, S.K. (eds.) Mobile Ad-hoc and Sensor Networks. MSN 2006. LNCS, vol. 4325, pp. 424–435. Springer, Berlin, Heidelberg (2006). https://doi.org/10.1007/11943952_36

19. Gomathi, K., Parvathavarthini, B.: An efficient cluster based key management scheme for MANET with authentication. In: Trendz in Information Sciences & Computing (TISC), pp. 202–205. IEEE (2010)

20. Abusalah, A., Khokhar, A., Guizani, A.: A survey of secure mobile adhoc routing protocols. IEEE Commun. Surv. Tutor. **10**(4), 78–93 (2008)

Developing a Conceptual Framework for Smart Education Environment Integrating IoT in Architectural Education Adapting Global Competence

Shanta Pragyan Dash(✉)

Centre for Socio-Architectural Studies, Manipal School of Architecture and Planning, Manipal Academy of Higher Education, Manipal, Karnataka, India
dashshanta5@gmail.com

Abstract. Information and communication technology (ICT) advancements have an impact on many aspects of life and society, including the educational system. A key component of smart cities and the educational system alike, the IoT (Internet of Things) is becoming increasingly crucial. The COVID-19 epidemic, which began in March 2020, has accelerated educational reform and compelled institutions of higher learning to integrate ICT. Despite this, the Internet of Things (IoT) is still in its infancy in the education system, and its influence is still largely unknown. The research is an attempt to explore the potential of IoT in architectural education pedagogy which is primarily relying on creativity and innovation. Re-thinking about the student-centered pedagogies which acquires critical thinking skills, polite communication skills, conflict resolution skills, perspective taking skills, and adaptability towards global competence is the demand of the time which is the focus of the research. The outcome of the article is to propose a conceptual framework for smart education environment integrating IoT in Architectural Education adapting Global Competence for the future generations.

Keywords: Information and communication technology · Internet of Things (IoT) · Architectural Education · Global Competence · Smart Education Environment

1 Introduction

1.1 An Overview of IoT

The Internet of Things (IoT) allows real and virtual things to communicate and collaborate. The Internet of Things (IoT) is a global network of interconnected devices and items that has gained traction in recent years. The Internet of Things allows items and people to be connected at any time and from any location, allowing for the identification, integration, and creation of global knowledge. In this context, institutions will need to focus their efforts on responding to the changing demands of the knowledge worker, new employment kinds, and the future economy [1]. Lifelong teaching, research, and learning activities must be integrated into higher education systems, both inside and across national educational systems and labor market tools. Simultaneously, the Internet of Things (IoT) will have an impact on education in a variety of ways, including technological (Cloud/Fog Computing, instructional technologies, mobile apps), educational reform, changes in teaching and learning, practical and experimental changes, campus [2, 3], security and confidentiality, quality and ethics, and financial changes. The Internet of Things enables educational stakeholders to translate data acquired by sensors and mobile devices into valuable information [4] and act on that information [5]. It is critical to investigate the influence of IoT adoption in education in order to completely appreciate its benefits and drawbacks [3]. Developing intelligent interactive classrooms, designing interactive models to engage students in the learning process, stimulating innovation, and delivering real-time reporting on students' cognitive activities [6]. The COVID-19 pandemic has affected both research and the application of innovative technology in education. The number of publications on the use of IoT in education has grown, and contemporary educational efforts reflect this interest [7].

1.2   Current Education System in Architectural Schools

The architectural education of first-year students was mostly theoretical and experimental in nature, with an emphasis on investigating design concepts through physical modelling and the creation of tangible design prototypes. Other technical subjects are also taught conceptually and through hand-drawn sheets during these early years. Since the epidemic and lockdowns began, the majority of classes have been switched to online lectures, and traditional methods of teaching these young kids will undergo a radical transformation. A novel approach must be used to ensure that the quality of education is not jeopardized for the incoming class. Many institutions still require students to use hand-drafted sheets and physical models to develop their creativity and imagination, so second-year students face the same challenges as their juniors. Other subjects are also taught without the use of computers and technology. Additionally, only a small percentage of first-year college students are outfitted with laptop computers. To make a significant impact on architectural education, it is imperative that all of the relevant elements be considered and a workable solution for students is developed. It may be a short-term fix, but if successful it could be used in the future, where technology plays a large role in education.

As the academic year progresses, many students have a better understanding of how the semester works and how to handle the complexities of college life. In the third year of college, students are expected to struggle the most, making it even more difficult for them to succeed. Lectures and other scholarly pursuits. The quality of education will suffer as a result of moving online, and students will miss out on a lot of the pleasure. Some crucial parts like case studies and site/market visits for research will be placed on hold, despite the fact that most of the subjects are technical and comprehensive. Fourth-year students, despite the fact that they face many of the same issues as the first-year students, may be more equipped for this situation. This class won't be adversely affected by the change, as nearly all of its members own laptop computers, and virtually all of the subjects it needs to cover can be taught online. Even though it's a critical year, many students will be working on large-scale projects and some schools will have final thesis projects, the new classroom can handle most of the work.

Students, instructors, and other members of the support staff will all have to adapt to the new ways of teaching and functioning in the future. Virtual classrooms, e-mails and juries for classwork submission and evaluation, and video conferencing for class discussions will be the new modes of lecture presentation. For the less tech-savvy students, this will be a new skill to learn. Change is an unavoidable fact of life. As a result of this epidemic, one unavoidable fact is that architecture education will and should undergo modifications in order to adjust to the new normal. It is difficult to predict what changes can be expected because a large number of factors must be addressed from a variety of perspectives. Without a doubt, technology will play a new and more important role in facilitating this transition. Therefore, the inclination towards digital mode of teaching and learning is eventually becoming the need of the time.

1.3 Inclination Towards Digital Mode of Teaching and Learning

Digital teaching and learning have exploded, especially in higher education [1]. The rising expense of higher education and advances in digital technologies are major factors [2]. Researches have shown that inefficient university management, desire to "buy the best", and supply-side issues/mismatches as important causes of rising education costs [4]. Several private companies provide online courses using their own platforms. Many government-approved educational institutes in India now provide blended and online courses to their learners [5]. The Indian government's digitalization effort has accelerated this development. These advances in India's IT competence almost dictate the pace of the digital education revolution [8].

Because educational demands are rapidly changing, it is crucial for institutions to identify the appropriate pedagogical tools and strategies in the new learning environment [9].However, there are several drawbacks to adopting a digital learning paradigm, such as the lack of faculty status, financial burden of program execution, and faculty insufficient knowledge [10]. An effective online learning platform requires a combination of uniformity and customization. The transition is rapid, and all stakeholders in educational institutions must recognize and prepare for the new era learning that began long ago and now requires technologically creative pedagogical inputs. In digital education, the focus shifts from the instructor to the student, according to research [11]. Many studies have focused on the core features and abilities required for a faculty to effectively teach online [12]. Adaptability, positivity, and confidence are personal attributes that e-moderators should cultivate, according to one research [13]. According to another study, competent online teachers play eight roles: process facilitator, advisor-counselor, assessor-researcher-content facilitator-technologist, designer, manager-administrator [7]. Thus, further study is required to discover the information, aptitude, and skills required to be a successful online instructor.

1.4 Transforming Learning Environments in Architecture Schools

Creative and adaptive teaching methods are growing popular in architectural schools [1]. Thus, understanding the importance of non-traditional teaching pedagogies is crucial. Interstitial learning spaces such as cafés, lounges, alcoves, and outdoor learning are also becoming more popular [14]. These settings have demonstrated to be more adaptable for students. It's a reflection of the belief that learning develops everywhere and at any time [15]. From school computer labs to personal PCs, wireless IT and face-to-face contact are becoming increasingly vital. People's affinity for computers has decreased with the advent of computers that resemble pencils [16]. However, adaptable learning settings with window displays and visual spreads are the new educational marketing trend [1]. Design studios, where architecture students learn the most, require the most space flexibility [17]. The design studio is an aberration within the institution, rather than a classroom or laboratory, where knowledge is created and received. Universities teaching "fine arts" may distance themselves from art schools, making it difficult for students to receive feedback on their work. For one, "practice" is defined, whereas "knowledge" is defined [18]. Architecture has never been detached from public life as long as it is perceived as having a substantial role in it. Architecture schools may educate other institutions how to create flexible and adaptive design studio learning environments. In a wonderful school, there is no castle, but rather a small city full of people engaged and connecting [19]. In education, competing opinions are discussed openly. Thus, formal and informal learning should be linked in an architectural school devoted to open exchange of ideas [20]. Unlike rigidity, resilience is a dynamic ability to adapt to change.

In the architecture program, we are transitioning from the ideal of a generic architect well-equipped for broad practice to the creation of a spectrum of different types of architects with distinct specialties [21]. Nowadays, most students enroll in architecture schools that focus on certain architectural processes like formal, social, or environmental design. These methods, however, can quickly deteriorate into beliefs that produce stiff graduate's incapable of fresh conceptualization[22]. A current trend is architectural specialties, where each student graduates with a unique combination of skills and expertise. These specializations include digital architecture, sustainable architecture, and history. Specialization requires architectural schools with 25–30 faculty members, but this must be weighed against the sense of isolation students have at institutions of this scale [23]. Architectural education is becoming increasingly specialized, as is research and its application in the classroom. Our view is that full-time academics should be actively involved in research and teaching cutting-edge concepts. Design research has recently acquired acceptance as a viable means of creating new knowledge. An important distinction between design and research should be made. All of these ideas may be modified and updated if we adapt to new teaching and learning settings that foster global competency abilities among graduates. For an architecture student to be creative, the learning environment must be flexible and adaptive.

1.5 Transformative Pedagogies for Architecture Schools Towards Promoting Global Competence

Student-centered pedagogies can help students acquire critical thinking skills, polite communication skills, conflict resolution skills, perspective taking skills, and adaptability. Studio projects involving group cooperation may assist students think critically and teamwork abilities [24]. Participants create their own learning materials, which they present and assess as a group. Topic- or theme-based exercises can accommodate student capabilities and ages. Collaborative learning requires learners to feel comfortable and secure, and the work and its goals must be clearly defined. In collaborative activities, students must be courteous, attentive, honest, and compassionate. Those that work together quickly realize this fact [25]. Students can collaborate both inside and outside the classroom. The instructor facilitates discussions where students can express cultural biases, prejudices, and differences of opinion. A movie, picture, or text that gets pupils thinking is a typical teaching tool. As a result of their observations and personal opinions, students may present proof [26].

Constructive critique via organized dialogues is gaining popularity in architecture education as a way to raise students' knowledge of global and multicultural challenges while also improving their communication and reasoning abilities. In the long run, it may be advantageous for pupils to express opposing ideas. Reflective discussion allows students to actively listen and constructively reply to their peers. There is no one right answer to a problem, and students learn in the classroom to understand why others have different viewpoints, to reflect on their own, and to communicate with others effectively [27]. Practical training through real-world community initiatives can also assist students develop global competencies. This includes students participating in organized activities that help their local communities and build on classroom learning [28]. Students are required to critically reflect on their service experiences afterward to better understand the course material and their own role in society in terms of civic, social, economic, and political problems [29]. What distinguishes practical learning from other community service and volunteerism is that it is curriculum-based. Students who participate in service learning not only "serve to learn", but also "learn to serve".

Around the world, schools are using Story Circles to teach students essential intercultural skills like respect, cultural self-awareness, and empathy while learning about diverse cultures [30]. Students in groups of 5–6 deliver a three-minute story from their own personal experience when asked specific questions such as "Tell us about your first meeting with someone who was different from you". During a "flashback" activity, students take turns sharing their most memorable personal recollections with the group. Intercultural contact can take many forms, including simulations, interviews, and role plays [31]. To improve self-awareness and design thinking abilities to provide unique solutions to recognized difficulties, the same approach may be implemented into architectural pedagogy. IoT being a new evolving tool in architectural education proves to be challenging as a part of architectural pedagogy.

1.6 Applications of IOT and Connected E-Learning

The term "Internet of Things" refers to the interconnectedness of things and their ability to communicate with each other (IoT). Sensors and actuators are built into the device, which may be used to collect data and exchange it with other devices [6]. The Internet of Things (IoT) can be seen as a step toward the Internet of Everything (IoE). According to the corporation 'Cisco', all of these items are well-known in the (IoT) internet of things sector. The network that links the items to connect with the internet is evaluated by context-awareness, energy independence, and an increase in power processing [2]. In time, it becomes (IoE) the Internet of Everything (IoE) because of the extra production of all the things. The Internet of Things (IoT) will be discussed briefly in the article's later parts. In this post, we'll focus on the specifics of e-learning and how the Internet of Things (IoT) fits into that process [4]. This section's quotations from prior works might be helpful when discussing the respective issues. (IoT) The Internet of things may be implemented by following the linked sequence of network-connected things. Additional IoT-enabled features like energy independence, context awareness, and a higher-power CPU can be added to the IoT platform to create the internet of everything (IoE). According to IoT study, 99.4% of distinct physical things may be represented in the same way [8]. The whitepaper that includes the saying claims that the Internet of Everything (IoE) is a significant step toward linking intelligent network connections that enables for the connectivity of all other network connections. It is reported that some of them are connected to the internet of things in school systems throughout the world [5]. The IoE's potential is being utilized across the world to create a strong relationship between education and the IoE. With IoT, students gain a foundational understanding of how to actively participate in their own education by using certain intrinsically motivating principles [4]. By using IoT, they are able to conduct in-depth research into specialized areas of study. Through a network of people, specific procedures, raw data and items that can be linked to liabilities with continual access and serve as a guarantee, it is possible to achieve the advantages. By recognizing the served hazards, educators and policymakers must be well-prepared to fight against exploitation [1]. According to the GSMA, the Internet of Things (IoT) can allow new kinds of life-improving services [4]. According to others, IoT's significant function in the education system may be defined as mobile-enabled solutions (Kalashnikov et al. 2017). It is essential and helpful for teachers to use a learning method that is tailored to each student's specific needs. When viewed from the perspective of physical or virtual classrooms, competency levels can be enhanced on an overall basis. By utilizing real or virtual classrooms, the Internet of Things (IoT) increases the efficiency of learning. Internet of Things (IOT) can operate as a foundation for smart ecosystems. For smart environments, it begins the process of item detection and identification [6]. The online retrieval of information may be made easier with the adaptive functionality. All students, even those who are merely using the internet, are expected to know where their information comes from. Education, business, transportation, agriculture, healthcare, and management are just a few examples of the wide variety of fields covered. In a broad sense, the subject of the Internet of Things is the focus of this article (IoT). E-learning is supposed to be used as a source of knowledge for its users. E-learning is a form of learning that is 'electronically supplied' and is therefore the "modified version of learning". Indulgence may be defined as the act of using one's computer in a way that suggests using the internet [8]. This type of E-learning process improvement approach benefits both students and teachers. For them, the E-LEARNING process begins the process of efficiency that becomes productive and beneficial. With the use of E-learning, students and teachers may interact more effectively in order to learn more effectively [2]. It is possible to improve the efficiency of e-learning by using the Internet of Things (IoT). Animations, online tutorials, study materials via virtual classrooms, video lectures and many more may be utilized as an e-learning technique. Since all these key attributes are a part of architectural pedagogy, it is possible to see that the IoT's approach to learning makes it effective. Maybe it can be done via virtual or physical classrooms that provide more ease and accessibility to e-learning.

2 Conceptual Framework

2.1 Smart Education Environment Integrating IoT in Architecture Schools

The Internet of Things (IoT) transforms every aspect of our lives by making every device smart. Similarly, one encounters a genuine chain in which energy cleverly moves from smart education, a smart university, an intelligent classroom, intelligent teaching, and intelligent learning all the way to smart evaluation. The following are the attributes to contribute towards developing a conceptual framework for integrating IoT for Smart education environments in architecture schools (Fig. 1).

2.2 Smart Education

Smart technologies such as cloud computing, big data, and the Internet of Things (IoT) allow for the transformation of education into smart education and play a significant part in creating a smart education environment. As a result of smart education, workers will be equipped with 21st century skills and knowledge to deal with the difficulties of the modern world. An IoT infrastructure, which includes sensors, user applications, and communication links, is essential to the realization of smart education. Teachers and students will benefit from IoT use in education because pupils learn more quickly and teaching staff will be able to carry out their duties more effectively.

2.3 Smart University

In order to be considered a "smart institution", a college or university must incorporate cutting-edge concepts, smart hardware and software, and smart classrooms outfitted with the newest technologies. An interactive learning environment, worldwide material access, and adaptive learning based on network data collection and analysis are all features of a smart university. In many colleges, the Internet of Things (IoT) is already present in the form of security cameras, temperature control systems, building access devices as well as electric and heating systems.

2.4 Smart Classrooms

The "Smart classroom" is a term that refers to a classroom that has a lot of electronic tools for teaching and learning, like digital displays, video projectors, and web-connected devices. In a "smart classroom", everything from class management to access to learning resources and interaction with other students is made possible and integrated with the context in which they happen. There were a lot of things that went into making the smart class in 2012, like video projectors, sensors, and facial recognition algorithms that keep an eye on a lot of different physical environment factors. The Internet of Things (IoT) connects smart devices together to make a smart class that can be accessed from any place at any time. In architecture, group works and case studies can be handled with such techniques. Those with limited mobility can learn at home with IoT-based learning systems, while those with impaired hearing can convert audio files into text and those with visual impairments can convert text into audio, implying that the IoT is able to meet some of their needs. People with disabilities can get a lot out of the Internet of Things (IoT), which is mostly reliant on connectivity. A smart class allows for more flexibility, knowledge exchange, better thinking skills, and more participation, to name a few.

2.5 Smart Teaching

The use of multiple technological devices to deliver material makes smart teaching distinct from more traditional methods. The information is accessible at any time, and the learning is personalized. By using sensing devices, the Internet of Things (IoT) may give students access to the real world, making instruction more difficult because it must be customized and adapted to meet the needs of students with disabilities (such as vision, hearing, or locomotion impairments or hyperactivity disorders). Since, architecture needs more verbal communication which involves one to one interaction with students for regular discussions, such technological devices for explaining the fundamentals, shall play a major role.

2.6 Smart Learning

Electronic gadgets are used to facilitate an adaptive learning process known as "smart learning". Smart learning is a method of learning that places the interests of both the student and the teacher at its center. It is less device-centric and relies on the ICT framework for its efficacy, smartness, and adaptability. A virtual classroom and a competitive learning environment can only be created with the help of IoT-based e-learning apps. This fosters online self-teaching (where architecture students are more engaged in self-learning and understanding), since students may connect to any lab or library in the globe so that they can conduct experiments, gather data, be given and submit homework or for self-assessments.

2.7 Smart Assessment

Multiple-choice tests and knowledge enhancement are two of the primary reasons why smart assessment is superior to traditional assessment techniques. For monitoring objects in smart environments, technology and the establishment of a true ecosystem are required. It is critical that modern learning systems include the appropriate capabilities for recording student behavior in online learning evaluation procedures. IoT devices may be used to assess how attentive pupils are in class, which is critical when evaluating education. Smart education necessitates the use of innovative teaching and learning methods, as well as new assessment methods and other factors. As a result, smart assessment should contain tools and procedures for identifying fraud and plagiarism, as well as scenarios in which students memorize answers to exercises that may only be used to demonstrate how well they know the content for an exam if they aren't utilized in the actual thing. Exams for bright children can also be modified based on how they respond to questions and presented in a style that they want to study. An investigation of this nature would allow researchers to examine how students comprehend and apply knowledge, as well as how they learn and how they learn best. While simulations may be used to put people to the test, they can also be utilized to assist people learn.

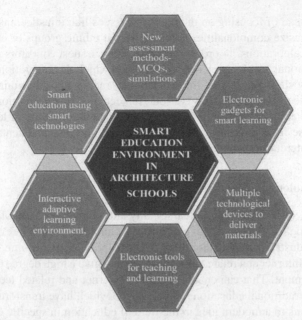

Fig. 1. Conceptual Framework for integrating IoT for Smart Education Environment in Architecture Schools

3 Discussion

3.1 Developing Values and Attitudes in Teaching that Promote Global Competency

An important first step in assisting students to build values that would allow them to prosper in a global environment is human rights and anti-discrimination education. The value of human dignity and cultural variety should be incorporated in all debate subjects, even though substantial progress has been made. It is possible for educators to use examples from many cultural backgrounds to demonstrate fundamental ideas and concepts, as well as to emphasize the contributions made by people of various ethnic origins to our collective knowledge and general quality of life. Instructors must have the ability and confidence to use a wide range of culturally diverse examples in the classroom on a frequent basis in order to be effective. Teachers and students communicate their beliefs and attitudes through their interactions, methods, and the behavior and perspectives for which they are rewarded in the classroom, as well as the official curriculum. Students are more likely to absorb the atmosphere of the classroom than they are to understand the topic in full detail. Since schools and classrooms have an important role in shaping students' values, educators who keep this in mind throughout their careers may be better able to assess the influence of their teaching on student values. For example, a teacher may re-think his or her classroom's seating arrangement in order to increase diversity in the classroom. Teachers, on the other hand, may find it difficult to openly discuss diversity and prejudice with their pupils. Disagreements about prejudice and ethics often flare up since most individuals aren't used to conversing with others who aren't like themselves. Instead of focusing on more serious issues like injustice, instructors might choose to emphasize commonalities across different ethnic groups or ethnic customs, costumes, and celebrations. In order to address these issues, educators need access to ongoing professional development opportunities for which the integration of IoT in education pedagogy shall play a vital role. To combat racism and discrimination, trainers can develop critical awareness of how various subject areas and instructional approaches can be used; the ability to recognize and accommodate the diversity of learners' needs, particularly those from minority groups; and a command of fundamental observation, listening, and intercultural communication techniques.

3.2   IoT Technology Benefits on E-learning

The educational system has been fundamentally altered by the advent of contemporary Internet technologies. The concept of ubiquitous technology has given several benefits to the education industry, including the ability to teach and study at any time, from any location. To say the Internet and related technologies may give a high degree of accessibility is an understatement. That can enable access to Internet and related technologies that have converted traditional education systems to the which have transformed traditional education systems to a modern idea in the field of education in specific e-learning. IoT application learning. Using Internet of Things (IoT) technologies in e-learning activities, students may connect with instructors by completing all assignments, online exams, and receiving results in real-time mode while working remotely.

3.3   Remote Access to LAB

The Internet of Things (IoT) is a great way to link physical and virtual devices. If a user (learner) wants to access the lab objects, they can do so over the Internet. Remote experimentation, data collection, and data receipt are all made feasible by IoT's design, which allows users to connect to their equipment from a distance. In addition, students or professors can use virtual labs to carry out their experiments remotely.

3.4   Real Time Access to Global Library

A global network of libraries is another framework built possible by the Internet of Things. The Internet of Things (IoT) makes it possible to access books and libraries, whether they are in hard copy or digital format. Students, researchers, and instructors may access libraries all around the world through an online global link. The Internet of Things (IoT) is a smart technology that can be incorporated into programs, processes, and systems, making them more efficient. With the Internet of Things, smarter access to the global library system is now possible. In this manner, students can have access to a huge number of university libraries throughout the clock in order to have access to online resources. Book collections and public libraries throughout the world are being linked together via the Internet of Things (IoT) and the technology that support it. This enables users to access the world's largest online library of books and knowledge resources.

3.5 Smart Collaboration

These kinds of infrastructure necessitate a collaborative system in the first place because of the prevalence of online learning. Different educational eco-systems can create an interactive platform by utilizing the online environment that enables IoT and the effective connection and communication between items. In collaborative environments for educational infrastructures, good communication is essential. A higher level of communication and engagement is possible because to the Internet of Things' hyper-connectivity and efficient communication between real and virtual devices. IoT provides a big, efficient collaboration platform that may be driven by smart technologies. These technologies enable correct and effective communication between virtual and physical devices via the Internet of Things. However, new Internet technologies that support the Internet of Things (IoT) can revolutionize the real idea of collaboration in e-learning. It is possible for internet users to learn more effectively, collaboratively, and actively in an Internet-of-things-enabled collaborative environment. In a smart collaborative environment, they may develop a better timetable for their activities. Smart methods of cooperation can also foster a more effective planning of teamwork.

The Internet of Things (IoT) has the potential to create a worldwide collaboration platform by linking a huge number of objects. It has the potential to spur team development on a massive scale, resulting in the formation of extremely large project groups, resulting in a deluge of interactions between the group and its many ideas and concepts. As well as inside national geo-graphical settings, students and teachers can operate within a global infrastructure. In general, the use of IoT tools, modules, and technologies may be regarded to be predictable and anticipated to improve significantly.

3.6 Online Self Learning

Students are encouraged to learn on their own through the use of self-learning or auto-didacticism. Students are more likely to complete their assignments on time when they use this study method since they are more self-motivated. Due to the advent of the Internet of Things (IoT), formerly non-interactive items are now capable of interacting with one another and assisting humans in their pursuit of knowledge on their own. Consider a scenario in which a university's campus has a few touchable wireless computers scattered throughout. It is possible for learners to engage with the computer in order to answer questions or construct queries. In order to gain access to the machine, the user must first pass an authentication procedure including physical scanning (fingerprint or RFID Card). Students may perform their assignments, collect resources, and email and receive assignments to their professors from anywhere, at any time. The Internet of Things (IoT) provides the ability to link any object to any other object at any time. Students can conduct experiments and get data from any lab or library (as previously described) by enrolling their mobile or physical credentials. Doing assignments and submitting them for evaluation is all part of the process. They might also receive exam results.

4 Conclusion

Being wise about higher education is a vital first step in adapting to today's knowledge-based, globally interconnected society. Because of the new conditions and limitations brought on by the COVID-19 pandemic, it is essential to use ICT as a foundation for implementing IoT and developing a new kind of smart education. The proliferation of IT infrastructures and information systems in architecture schools can also contribute to the emergence of vulnerabilities. The widespread use of the Internet of Things (IoT) as an educational technology/instrument necessitates significant caution in guaranteeing data security and integrity, as well as particular disaster recovery processes. It is important to evaluate these aspects in light of the damage that malicious software efforts might do to essential IT systems, such as banking and security systems, education and health-care systems, etc. There was an increase in the number of cyberattacks on educational institutions during the pandemic period when most operations were conducted remotely and via the use of ICTs. In light of the infancy of ITC adoption and the transition to the Internet of Things in higher education in many countries, new information regarding the adoption of the IoT in universities and the transition to a smart university is challenging and vital.

References

1. Soni, V.D.: IOT connected with e-learning. Int. J. Integr. Educ. **2**(5), 273–277 (2019)
2. Sharma, P., Agrawal, A.: A study of internet of things: architectural perspective. Int. J. Emerg. Res. Manag. Technol. **6**(8), 351 (2018). https://doi.org/10.23956/ijermt.v6i8.165
3. Chawla, S., Tomar, D.P., Gambhir, D.S.: Smart education: a proposed IoT based interoperable architecture to make real time decisions in higher education. Rev. Gestão Inovação Tecnol. **11**(4), 5643–5658 (2021). https://doi.org/10.47059/revistageintec.v11i4.2589
4. Sharma, M., Dwivedi, A., Sengar, A., Solanki, M.: Implementing innovative online teaching-learning practice in higher education: understanding student perspective. In: ACM International Conference on Proceeding Series, pp. 136–140 (2020). https://doi.org/10.1145/337 7571.3377577
5. Bayani, M., Leiton, K., Loaiza, M.: Internet of things (IoT) advantages on e-learning in the smart cities IoT-based library automation & monitoring system view project internet of things (IOT) advantages on e-learning in the smart cities. Int. J. Dev. Res. **07**(January), 17747–17753 (2017). http://www.journalijdr.com
6. Bennett, S., Lockyer, L.: Becoming an online teacher: adapting to a changed environment for teaching and learning in higher education. EMI. Educ. Media Int. **41**(3), 231–248 (2004). https://doi.org/10.1080/09523980410001680842
7. Mircea, M., Stoica, M., Ghilic-Micu, B.: Investigating the impact of the internet of things in higher education environment. IEEE Access **9**, 33396–33409 (2021). https://doi.org/10.1109/ACCESS.2021.3060964
8. Kassab, M., DeFranco, J., Laplante, P.: A systematic literature review on Internet of things in education: benefits and challenges. J. Comput. Assist. Learn. **36**(2), 115–127 (2020). https://doi.org/10.1111/jcal.12383
9. IOT Application in Education - IJARnD. https://www.ijarnd.com/manuscript/iot-application-in-education/. Accessed 15 Feb 2022
10. Pai, S.S., Vikhyath, Shivani, Sanket, Shruti: IOT application in education. Int. J. Adv. Res. Dev. **2**(6), 20–24 (2017). xx.xxx/ijariit-v2i6-1148
11. IEEE Xplore Full-Text PDF. https://ieeexplore.ieee.org/stamp/stamp.jsp?arnumber=935 9788. Accessed 15 Feb 2022
12. Aldowah, H., Ul Rehman, S., Ghazal, S., Naufal Umar, I.: Internet of things in higher education: a study on future learning. J. Phys. Conf. Ser. **892**(1), 012017 (2017). https://doi.org/10.1088/1742-6596/892/1/012017

13. Afrin, S., Chowdhury, F.J., Rahman, M.M.: COVID-19 pandemic: rethinking strategies for resilient urban design, perceptions, and planning. Front. Sustain. Cities 32 (2021). https://doi.org/10.3389/FRSC.2021.668263

14. Markusen, A.: Creative placemaking. http://arts.gov/pub/pubDesign.php. Accessed 08 Feb 2022

15. Sepe, M.: The role of public space to achieve urban happiness. Int. J. Sustain. Dev. Plan. 12(4), 724–733 (2017). https://doi.org/10.2495/SDP-V12-N4-724-733

16. Williams, D.R.: Making sense of 'place': reflections on pluralism and positionality in place research. Landsc. Urban Plan. 131, 74–82 (2014). https://doi.org/10.1016/J.LANDURBPLAN.2014.08.002

17. Inishev, I.: Embedded creativity: Structural interconnections between materiality, visuality, and agency in everyday perceptual settings. Creat. Stud. 11(1), 70–84 (2018). https://doi.org/10.3846/cs.2018.541

18. Brown, B.B., Perkins, D.D.: Disruptions in place attachment. In: Altman, I., Low, S.M. (eds.) Place Attachment. Human Behavior and Environment, vol. 12, pp. 279–304. Springer, Boston (1992). https://doi.org/10.1007/978-1-4684-8753-4_13

19. Dash, S.P.: A sustainable approach towards development of an island community. J. Civ. Eng. Environ. Technol. 4(1), 32–38 (2017). https://www.krishisanskriti.org/vol_image/10Aug201712080910ShantaPragyanDash32-38.pdf

20. Fornell, C., Larcker, D.F.: Evaluating structural equation models with unobservable variables and measurement error. J. Mark. Res. 18(1), 39–50 (1981)

21. Dash, S.P.: Behavioural impact of interior landscaping on human psychology. Int. J. Civ. Eng. Technol. 9(2), 661–674 (2018)

22. Salizzoni, E., Pérez-Campaña, R.: Design for biodiverse urban landscapes: connecting place-making to place-keeping. Ri-Vista 18(2), 130–149 (2019). https://doi.org/10.13128/rv-7641

23. Aflaki, A., Mahyuddin, N., Samzadeh, M., Mirnezhad, M.: The influence of place making's attributes on the resident's usage and satisfaction in high-rise residential community: a case study. In: MATEC Web Conference, vol. 66 (2016). https://doi.org/10.1051/matecconf/20166600006

24. Furlan, R., Petruccioli, A., Jamaleddin, M.: The authenticity of place-making: space and character of the regenerated historic district in Msheireb, downtown Doha (state of Qatar). Archnet-IJAR 13(1), 151–168 (2019). https://doi.org/10.1108/ARCH-11-2018-0009

25. Kaftangui, M., Welling, B., Masalmeh, H., Anbar, Y.: Sustainable open public spaces: place making strategy for the breakwater 'al Kaser', Abu Dhabi. In: IOP Conference Series: Materials Science and Engineering, vol. 520, no. 1 (2019). https://doi.org/10.1088/1757-899X/520/1/012021

26. Putra, B.D., Horne, R., Hurley, J.: Place, space and identity through greening in Kampung Kota. J. Reg. City Plan. 30(3), 211–223 (2019). https://doi.org/10.5614/jpwk.2019.30.3.3

27. Avashia, V., Garg, A., Dholakia, H.: Understanding temperature related health risk in context of urban land use changes. Landsc. Urban Plan. 212, 104107 (2021). https://doi.org/10.1016/j.landurbplan.2021.104107

28. Yalçinalp, E., Şivil, M., Meral, A., Demir, Y.: Green roof plant responses to greywater irrigation. Appl. Ecol. Environ. Res. 17(2), 3667–3680 (2019). https://doi.org/10.15666/aeer/1702_36673680

29. Wentz, E.A., Rode, S., Li, X., Tellman, E.M., Turner, B.L.: Impact of homeowner association (HOA) landscaping guidelines on residential water use. Water Resour. Res. 52(5), 3373–3386 (2016). https://doi.org/10.1002/2015WR018238

30. Chitgopkar, S., Dash, S.P., Walimbe, S.: Gated community living: a study of contemporary residential development approach in Indian cities. PalArch's J. Archaeol. Egypt/Egyptol. **17**(9), 7437–7451 (2020)
31. Zawadzka, J.E., Harris, J.A., Corstanje, R.: A simple method for determination of fine resolution urban form patterns with distinct thermal properties using class-level landscape metrics. Landsc. Ecol. **36**(7), 1863–1876 (2020). https://doi.org/10.1007/s10980-020-01156-9

Energy Bill Minimisation of Dynamic Tariff Bound Residential Consumers by Intentional Load Shifting

Hithu Anand[1] , M. Rajalakshmi[2], G. R. Venkatakrishnan[1] , R. Rengaraj[1](✉) ,
and R. Jeya[2]

[1] Sri Sivasubramaniya Nadar College of Engineering, Chennai 603 110, India
rengarajr@ssn.edu.in
[2] SRM Institute of Science and Technology, Kattangalathur, Chennai, India

Abstract. Energy consumption and power demands are always in an increasing trend. Smart grid technologies like demand response (DR), demand side management (DSM) and dynamic pricing are possible only with internet-of-things (IoTs). Further, smart grid technologies are promising to alleviate distribution congestion and bring energy economy to consumers. However, these technologies can agitate consumer's choice of comfort and cause unexpected energy billing. Hence, a wide acceptance for DSM, DR among consumers, has become a challenge to power engineers and distribution companies. So, benefits due to load shifting in a dynamic tariff bound residential customer is analysed for single day. An automatic load shifting for energy economy with manual settings, without compromising consumer energy balance is analysed. From the results, it is justifiable as an acceptable solution for future smart grid. After load shifting, minimal energy billing cost without compromising consumer comfort and utility constraints are obtained. Hence, an active participation from the consumers can also be anticipated. IoTs and smart devices based prototype implementation is aimed as future work.

Keywords: Appliance scheduling · Demand Response · Demand Side Management · Energy economics · Internet of Things · Load shifting · Real Time Pricing · Smart grid technologies · Tariff

1 Introduction

Dynamic pricing technology is nearing to its implementation under smart grid pilot projects in India. Under smart grid pilot project, residential energy meters are already been converted to smart-meters (SMs) in many places. These SMs are capable of providing real time energy consumption data to state load dispatch centres (SLDCs). By the introduction of SMs, energy theft is mitigated and huge improvement in the commercial efficiency is observed. In Puducherry, [19] it claims an improvement of 65% energy efficiency and usage due to SMs. Smart grid technologies like demand side management (DSM), demand response (DR) and dynamic pricing like real time pricing (RTP) are

R. Venkataraman et al. (Eds.): ICIoT 2022, CCIS 1727, pp. 79–92, 2023.
https://doi.org/10.1007/978-3-031-28475-5_8

a part of SMs functionality. Indian electricity sector is nearing to quarter (25%) with residential energy demands, 18% in agricultural and 43% in industrial, commercial is 8% and traction loads are nearing to 2%. Revenue is generated by formulating heavy tariff schemes from commercial and industrial (C&I) loads or consumers. In energy market, though the generation or purchase-cost of energy is higher, electricity tariff lies under the monopoly of state government. Therefore, residential energy tariff is often politicised, especially in the interest of ruling party to get attention from general public. Hence, residential consumers mostly enjoy a subsidised tariff based on their usage. Such an approach will encourage freedom in a common scenario among the consumers. That is, inefficient and excessive usage of energy should be mitigated. It is also important to bring awareness among consumers that, electric energy is similar to water resource. Hence, adequate control of energy usage is possible only with the introduction of smart grid technologies.

Consumers side generation is encouraged hence, consumer turning into prosumers will cause surplus power available at the distribution networks (DNs). Hence, new tariff schemes in favour to prosumers should be implemented. Further, roof-top-solar (RTS) generation depends on solar availability and, peakload-time falls under a different time frame. Hence, a dynamic pricing scheme is required for DNs with residential prosumers. This will bring, reduced DN congestion and economy to keen energy conscious individuals etc. Further, a tremendous control over consumer consumption behaviour is made available to utility. Indirectly, distribution load control falls under SLDCs with a provision to curtail load on emergency scenarios. However, it will harm the comfort of consumers. So by dynamic pricing, consumer seeking energy economy will try to minimise their consumption at peak hours. The problem arisen is solved using automatic shifting of heavy shiftable loads. Hence, an automatic shifting of loads to less taxing time frame is the research interest. We formulate appliance scheduling problem into a mixed-integer linear programming (MILP) problem in general algebraic modelling system (GAMS). State-of-the-art IBM ILOG CPLEX optimiser is used to achieve optimal scheduling of appliances [1]. Ten appliances including electric vehicle (EV), is solved for optimal scheduling in a day. Similar to this, a quick reference to IoT based optimal DSM for smart micro-grid is given in [25]. Further, an overview of smart grid with smart meters and IoT enabled devices is given in [3].

2 Literature Survey

Agricultural loads are seasonal and sometimes even unexpected in DNs. These loads usually follow flat pricing schemes due to their constant load profiles such as pump load or mills. This unexpected loads can cause peak loading, increased power losses, congestion, increased demand of generation etc. Hence, at DNs, residential consumers are encouraged to contribute by local generation with RTS installations. India has already crossed 4.4 GW solar photo-voltaic (PV) installation [2] as on march 2019. Further, Indian government has made an ambitious target of 175 GW of renewable energy sources (RESs) by 2022 and 450 GW by 2030. Out of 175 GW RESs, 100 GW is PV based and 40 GW is RTS PV generation [14].

Real time pricing is a dynamic pricing strategy, such a pricing is given in [6]. Incentive is given to consumers based on renewable power generation. Indian pricing of dynamic tariff in this research is referred from [9]. Appliances are turned OFF at high pricing time-slots. So, problems arisen due to ON OFF state of appliances are binary in nature. Hence, MILP approach is made to such problems. Branch and bound (B&B) algorithm in solving a MILP problem of appliance scheduling with PV is given by [15]. Comfort is set to maximum for the problem. Another problem for minimising energy cost and reduction of peak load with PV integration is solved as B&B approach in [23]. Reduction in electricity bill is claimed and excess power from PV is send to national grid. A combination of seven home appliances are considered for the analysis. Further, fifteen appliances along with PV for energy schedule in a residential community is given in [18]. The ToU scenario is solved for optimal energy scheduling using GAMS CPLEX solver. Considerable reduction in total electricity cost is observed with PV power injecting to the grid.

Appliance scheduling is a large constrained optimisation problem. Aggregate scheduling of appliances will bring considerable DR benefit to utility. DR among 100 consumers is discussed in [8]. Economy is electricity bill and CO_2 emission reduction is claimed with a simulation study. ON OFF state of appliances is solved as 0/1 Knapsack problem. Implementation of such scheduling will require IoT based hardware infrastructure. An IoT based DSM in a smart grid is discussed in [25]. An advanced DSM for efficient management and control of smart micro-grid is discussed. The proposed scheme is claimed to have reduced energy cost, emission cost and peak-to-average ratio (PAR) in the micro-grid. Further, an overview to smart meters and IoT enabled devices in a smart grid is given in [3]. Focus is made on power quality and reliability monitoring. The review further focus on wireless communication, routing algorithms, open research issues etc. Smart grid technologies will ultimately contribute to a smarter city. In a smart city all resources will be optimally utilised. Energy, water optimisation, transportation, waste management and reduced emission etc. Energy, water optimisation and reduced emission using multi-objective MILP is given in [12]. Using GAMS environment energy use, water use and CO_2 emission is claimed to decrease by 47–94.7%, 20–100%, and 52–96% respectively. Information gap decision theory (IGDT) to address the EV charging, that is vehicle to grid (V2G) and grid to vehicle (G2V) is discussed in [22]. The non-linearity, uncertainty arisen due to price and charging is solved using GAMS CPLEX solver. Non-linear problem is approximated into linear problem to solve the complete problem as a MILP problem. Further, focusing on power and energy problems, its solutions in GAMS is given in [26].

Genetic algorithm (GA) to shift load and bring energy economy is discussed in [27]. GA is claimed to give better solution than MILP in the study. Home energy management system (HEMS) with energy storage system (ESS), wind turbine (WT), solar PV, micro gas turbine (MGT) and EV as a MILP is solved in [7]. RTP tariff for reduction in PAR ratio and energy economy is discussed. Considering demand forecast and RTP, an optimal heating ventilation and air-conditioning (HVAC) system with real time scheduling is given in [24]. Power units and appliances scheduling with HEMS is given in [17]. The MILP is solved and claimed to reduce electricity cost and peak demand. Monte Carlo simulation to depicts price uncertainty, outdoor temperature, RES generation, water usage and uncontrollable loads are given in [16]. Problem is essentially a MILP problem and solved for optimal schedule. A micro-grid consisting of ESS, RESs and load is solved as a MILP in [20]. An energy management system (EMS) is implemented and tested for an existing micro-grid at Aalborg University. Further, EMS in scheduling ESS, PV, generating units and load is given in [11]. An MILP, dynamic programming and minimum cut algorithm for appliances and battery scheduling of an active apartment building in Royal Seaport project in Stockholm is given in [21]. Electricity bill reduction and CO_2 emission reduction is claimed.

Smart HEM with EV, V2G, G2V and energy trading is solved as MILP in [13]. RTP along with peak reduction DR scenarios for four-member Portuguese family house is studied. Electricity cost reduction efficiency of 65% is claimed in the study. Facilitating increased penetration of RESs into a micro-grid by DR and ESS coordination is explained in [4]. Problem is solved using GAMS CPLEX solver to optimise overall operation of islanded micro-grid. Classifying appliances as deferrable/non-deferrable and interruptible/non-interruptible to optimise its schedule is given in [10]. Worst case RTP fluctuation is considered to give robust solution with MILP approach.

2.1 Assumptions

In this paper, certain assumptions are made in order to bring simplicity without compromising quality and intended objectives. Each appliances are assumed to have its own fixed power consumption levels. All connected "type" of appliances are turned ON at a time and, appliances once turned ON are assumed to operate at-least for an hour. According to consumer comfort, these appliances are classified as shiftable (S), non-shiftable (NS) and shifted-to-limited time-slots (SL) settings. Hence, a pre-defined energy consumption value is available.

3 Methodology

Under dynamic pricing, residential loads are shifted to lower pricing slot to bring energy bill economy for single day. Based on flat tariff, RTP and time of use (ToU) tariffs are compared. A typical Indian residential layout is given in Fig. 1 and appliance rating are tabulated in Table 1 [5]. Residential light load (LL) is rated for full load ampere (FLA) of 6A and power load (PL) for 16A FLA respectively. Air-conditioning (AC) device specification is calculated based on floor size. From the residential layout in Fig. 1, all rooms falls within the range of $100\,ft^2$ to $200\,ft^2$. Hence, an AC of one ton capacity with 12000 British thermal unit (BTU) can be used, it will have a wattage of 1 kW. As per calculations, floor areas of $150.694\,ft^2$ is identified for two rooms each and $129.166\,ft^2$ for another room. This resulted in the installation of three AC devices of 1 kW each for all rooms. Power devices like AC, Water heater (WH), Washing Machine (WM), Refrigerator (REF), Pump (PM) and electric vehicle (EV) are connected to 16A sockets. These sockets are equipped with smartconversion-plug, wirelessly connected via smart meters, to enable DR in the residence. Appliances categories falls in set S, NS and SL are given below.

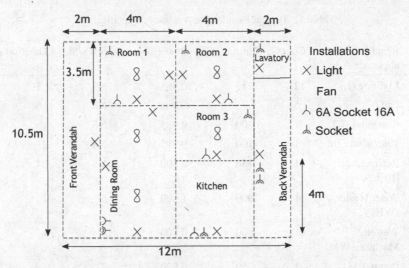

Fig. 1. Typical Indian Residential Layout with Electrical Installations

3.1 Formulation and Appliances Data

Appliances are in a set A as given in Eq. (1), for all time period i in T. Energy bill minimisation problem with objective function can be formulated as Eq. (1) meeting energy balance and maximum demand (MD) constraints. For each hour i, hourly price is given by C_i, appliance type j with power level $P_{i,j}$ is classified as completely shiftable P^S, shifted-to-limited time-slot $P^{SL}_{k,j}$ and non-shiftable P^{NS}_{ij}. Cumulative energy is limited to 36.650 kWh per day and hourly MD as 6.780 kW given by equality and inequality constraints respectively. x_i is the ON OFF state and, the problem is binary in nature, solved as MILP to minimise energy bill for electricity usage in a typical Indian residence.

Equation (1) gives energy bill minimisation objective of shiftable P^S, shiftableto-limited time-slot $P^{SL}_{k,j}$ and non-shiftable P^{NS}_{ij} appliances with hourly price C_i.

For hourly slot i in time T, appliances are in a set A.

Table 1. Typical Residential Appliance Specification

Sl No.	Residential appliances (A)	Count	Rating (W)	Power Factor	S/NS/SL	Duration (h)
1	Lighting (L)	12	15	0.985	NS	5
2	Fan (F)	5	75	0.800	NS	16
3	Computer (C)	1	200	0.985	NS	1
4	Television (TV)	1	100	0.985	NS	2
5	Refrigerator (REF)	1	150	0.800	NS	24
6	Water Heater (WH)	1	2000	1.000	S	1
7	Washing Machine (WM)	1	400	0.800	S	1
8	Pump (PM)	1	750	0.800	S	1
9	Electric Vehicle (EV)	1	750	1.000	SL	10
10	Air-Conditioner (AC)	3	1000	0.800	SL	5

$$\text{minimize} \quad E_c = \sum_{i=1}^{T} \sum_{j=1}^{A} CP_{ij}^{NS} x_i + \sum_{i=1}^{T} \sum_{j=1}^{A} CP_{ij}^{S} x_j$$

$$+ \sum_{i=1}^{T} \sum_{j=1}^{A} C_k P_{kj}^{SL} x_k$$

$$\text{subject to} \quad \sum_{i=1}^{T} \sum_{j=1}^{A} P_{ij} x_i = E \quad \forall i \in T, \forall j \in A \tag{1}$$

$$\sum_{j=1}^{A} P_{ij} x_i \leq MD \quad \exists! i \in T, \forall j \in A$$

$$x_i \in \{0, 1\} \quad \forall i \in T$$

$$k \in K, K \subset T$$

Note that, k belongs to K and K is a subset of T. Energy balance and MD constraints are also formulated above. Equality and inequality constrain of energy balance and MD for the day respectively. Hence, energy demand per day of the residential consumer is met without crossing the MD limit. Binary variable x_i decides the ON OFF state of connected appliances. Hence, the problem is solved as MILP problem with energy cost minimisation while meeting the energy balance, power demand and MD limitation.

Residential MD is calculated based on 66% of total current demand from lighting load, 100% demand of WH, AC up to 10 A, 100% demand of largest available sub-circuit and 40% demand of every other circuit. Hence, MD value of 6.780 kW is taken. Since the comparison is made between Flat pricing, ToU and RTP, MD is considered only in dynamic pricing scenario of RTP. RTP is hourly change in energy pricing. It can be proved that, MD and RTP has a strong correlation in terms of pricing or penalty.

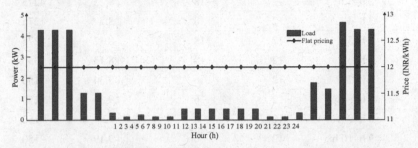

Fig. 2. Typical Indian residential load profile and existing pricing

3.2 Load Profile and Pricing Data

Each year, residential energy demand is increasing and new tariff is put forward by utilities. Soon flat tariff followed by present residential scenario will turn into dynamic pricing. Hence, a flat tariff of 12 INR (Indian Rupee) is taken with the load profile as given in Table 2. Various tariff schemes such as, flat, ToU and RTP are also tabulated in Table 2. RTP tariff is referred from [9]. Being a tropical country, most of the time in a year, residential demand is high in the evening hours and throughout the night. This is due to human presence in after office hours and dependence of electric appliances during these hours. Typically AC is turned ON only during sleeping hours. Hence, a typical load profile with flat tariff and usage in a typical day is depicted in Fig. 2. Note that, on the day energy pricing with flat tariff is 438.60 INR.

Hence, with flat tariff, possibility of demand response (DR) is nil. To alleviate peak demand, dynamic tariff should be introduced. Dynamic tariff depends on aggregate residential demand profile or combination of overall load profile including agricultural, C&I installations.

4 Result Summary and Discussion

Load shifting objective of MILP for ToU, RTP and MD constraints are solved value of 12 INR for the day. Taking residential profile into consideration, ToU with two period tariff is followed in this paper. A pricing of 6 INR from 6 h to using GAMS environment with CPLEX solver. All the tariffs will give an average 18 h and 18 INR from 18 h to 6 h as shown in the Fig. 3. Load is shifted for this tariff and on the day energy pricing after load shifting is obtained to be 401.54 INR with ToU.

Table 2. Hourly load, flat and dynamic pricing

Hours (h)	Time Slots (h)	Flat Pricing (Rs/kWh)	ToU (Rs/kWh)	RTP (Rs/kWh)	Load (W)
1	24 h–1 h	12	18	8.69	4275
2	1 h–2 h	12	18	8.13	4275
3	2 h–3 h	12	18	8.25	4275
4	3 h–4 h	12	18	8.5	1275
5	4 h–5 h	12	18	8.12	1275
6	5 h–6 h	12	18	8.13	330
7	6 h–7 h	12	6	8.34	150
8	7 h–8 h	12	6	9.35	250
9	8 h–9 h	12	6	12	150
10	9 h–10 h	12	6	9.19	150
11	10 h–11 h	12	6	12.23	525
12	11 h–12 h	12	6	20.61	525
13	12 h–13 h	12	6	26.82	525
14	13 h–14 h	12	6	27.35	525
15	14 h–15 h	12	6	13.81	525
16	15 h–16 h	12	6	17.31	525
17	16 h–17 h	12	6	16.42	150
18	17 h–18 h	12	6	9.83	150
19	18 h–19 h	12	18	8.63	330
20	19 h–20 h	12	18	8.87	1755
21	20 h–21 h	12	18	8.35	1455
22	21 h–22 h	12	18	16.44	4605
23	22 h–23 h	12	18	16.19	4275
24	23 h–24 h	12	18	8.87	4275

Indian electricity tariff schemes for residential sectors varies from state to state. It become difficult to find an average value of energy cost per unit. However, for each year, general trend is an increased cost of energy cost per unit.

Hence, flat tariff of 12 INR per unit is fixed to calculate the energy price for any given demand. ToU is assigned based on load profile and averaging 12 INR per unit per day and, RTP rates are referred from [9]. Hence, pricing profiles are based on Indian scenario of flat tariff, ToU and RTP.

Is turned ON only during 22 h to 5 h time-slots. Similarly, EV is put in dragging mode for 18 h to 6 h time-slots. Hence, they are in set SL. Further, duration of Initial ON

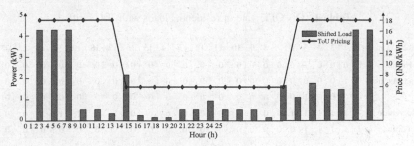

Fig. 3. Shifted residential load with ToU

Table 3. Initial ON OFF state of residential load with flat tariff

Appliances\Time	1	2	3	4	5	6	7	8	9	10	11	12	13	14	15	16	17	18	19	20	21	22	23	24
Lighting (L)	0	0	0	0	0	1	0	0	0	0	0	0	0	0	0	0	0	0	0	1	1	1	0	0
Fan (F)	1	1	1	1	1	0	0	0	0	0	1	1	1	1	1	1	0	0	0	1	1	1	1	1
Computer (C)	0	0	0	0	0	0	0	0	0	0	0	0	0	0	0	0	0	0	0	1	0	0	0	0
Televison (TV)	0	0	0	0	0	0	0	1	0	0	0	0	0	0	0	0	0	0	0	1	0	0	0	0
Refrigerator (REF)	1	1	1	1	1	1	1	1	1	1	1	1	1	1	1	1	1	1	1	1	1	1	1	1
Water Heater (WH)	0	0	0	0	0	0	0	0	0	0	0	0	0	0	0	0	0	0	0	0	0	1	0	0
Washing Machine (WM)	0	0	0	0	0	0	0	0	0	0	0	0	0	0	0	0	0	0	0	0	0	1	0	0
Pump (PM)	0	0	0	0	0	0	0	0	0	0	0	0	0	0	0	0	0	0	0	0	0	1	0	0
Electric Vehicle (EV)	1	1	1	1	1	0	0	0	0	0	0	0	0	0	0	0	0	0	0	1	1	1	1	1
Air-Conditioner (AC)	1	1	1	0	0	0	0	0	0	0	0	0	0	0	0	0	0	0	0	0	0	0	1	1

OFF state of all the appliances are given in Table 3. Note that, AC usage is mandatory for five hours and EV charging duration is made for ten hours respectively.

ON OFF state of P^S and P^{SL} appliances after shifting with respect to various tariff schemes are shown in Table 4, Table 5 and Table 6 respectively. This results give energy economy achievement of dynamic tariff bound residential consumer without compromising their comfort.

Table 4. ON OFF state of residential loads with ToU tariff

Appliances\Time	1	2	3	4	5	6	7	8	9	10	11	12	13	14	15	16	17	18	19	20	21	22	23	24
Water Heater	0	0	0	0	1	0	0	0	0	0	0	0	0	0	0	0	0	0	0	0	0	0	0	0
Washing Machine	0	1	0	0	0	0	0	0	0	0	0	0	0	0	0	0	0	0	0	0	0	0	0	0
Pump	0	0	0	0	1	0	0	0	0	0	0	0	0	0	0	0	0	0	0	0	0	0	0	0
Electric Vehicle	1	1	1	1	1	1	0	0	0	0	0	0	0	0	0	0	0	0	1	1	1	0	0	1
Air-Conditioner	1	1	1	1	1	0	0	0	0	0	0	0	0	0	0	0	0	0	0	0	0	0	0	0

Table 5. ON OFF state of residential loads with RTP based tariff

Appliances\Time	1	2	3	4	5	6	7	8	9	10	11	12	13	14	15	16	17	18	19	20	21	22	23	24
Water Heater	0	0	0	0	0	0	0	1	0	0	0	0	0	0	0	0	0	0	0	0	0	0	0	0
Washing Machine	0	0	0	0	0	0	0	0	0	0	0	0	0	1	0	0	0	0	0	0	0	0	0	0
Pump	0	0	0	0	0	0	0	0	0	0	0	0	0	0	0	0	0	0	1	0	0	0	0	0
Electric Vehicle	1	1	1	0	0	0	0	0	0	0	0	0	0	0	0	0	0	0	1	1	1	1	1	1
Air-Conditioner	1	1	1	0	0	0	0	0	0	0	0	0	0	0	0	0	0	0	0	0	0	0	1	1

Dynamic tariff of RTP will shift the load in obtaining energy economy of 353.75 INR. Same is shown in Fig. 4. However, load is nearing to MD and it should also be considered. Not considering MD might accumulate heavy load at any low pricing hour. To avoid this, the problem is solved taking considering MD constrain.

Economy of 355.24 INR is obtained. For the same, shifted load profile and pricing is shown in Fig. 5. Maximum demand of 6.780 kW is also depicted in the figure. Hence, after shifting P^S and P^{SL} with MD limitation for RTP, an energy A daily energy price of 438.60 INR for the energy consumption of 36.650 kWh per day is observed in flat pricing scheme. Typical loads like AC, WM, WH etc. are turned ON at the evening hours. This will give peak hours from early evening till late night. Hence, for tariffs like ToU and RTP, peak pricing is expected in these hours. By following ToU tariff, 401.54 INR is observed after RTP and RTP with MD penalty is 353.75 INR and 355.24 INR respectively. Load shifting. Further, for RTP tariff, energy pricing for load shifted based on Fig. 5 gives RTP with MD limit after load shifting.

Table 6. ON OFF state of residential loads with RTP having MD limitation

Appliances\Time	1	2	3	4	5	6	7	8	9	10	11	12	13	14	15	16	17	18	19	20	21	22	23	24
Water Heater	0	0	0	0	0	0	0	0	0	0	0	0	0	0	0	0	0	0	0	0	0	0	0	1
Washing Machine	0	1	0	0	0	0	0	0	0	0	0	0	0	0	0	0	0	0	0	0	0	0	0	0
Pump	0	0	0	0	1	0	0	0	0	0	0	0	0	0	0	0	0	0	0	0	0	0	0	0
Electric Vehicle	1	1	1	1	1	1	0	0	0	0	0	0	0	0	0	0	0	0	1	1	1	0	0	1
Air-Conditioner	1	1	1	1	1	0	0	0	0	0	0	0	0	0	0	0	0	0	0	0	0	0	0	0

Table 7. Pricing comparison

Pricing method	Flat (INR)	ToU (INR)	RTP (INR)	RTP (INR) with MD
Energy pricing per day	438.60	401.54	353.75	355.24

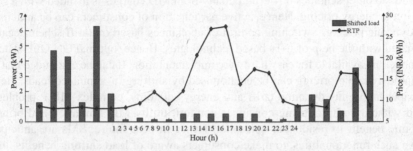

Fig. 4. Shifted residential load with RTP

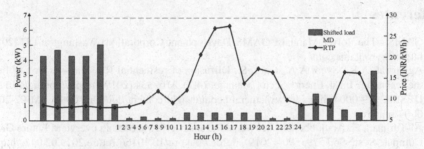

Fig. 5. Shifted residential load with RTP considering MD

Hence, energy economy is given with various tariff for the same energy consumption of the day. Same is tabulated in Table 7 as summary. Comparing to flat tariff, ToU has experienced 9.22% gain and RTP with 23.98% gain. Shifting a load with MD constrain is also economic with a gain of 23.46%. It is clear that, energy bill can be significantly minimised by residential consumers, if dynamic tariff is followed. Further, dynamic pricing can bring significant economy to residential consumers with active participation. This can alleviate peak loading within DNs with unexpected load burden or excess power demands.

5 Conclusion

Residential energy bill minimisation with dynamic tariffs in comparison to flat tariff is discussed. Significant energy bill minimisation of residential consumer, by intentional load shifting is achieved. Comparison is made among flat pricing, time of usage pricing, RTP and RTP with MD in-order to study the pricing economy, for same energy consumption. Dynamic pricing under utility control can introduce smart grid technologies like

DR and DSM. Hence, smart meters to record hourly consumption favouring dynamic tariff functionality should be aimed. Resulting economy in energy bill due to dynamic tariff will encourage wide acceptance of DSM and DR among consumers. So, benefits due to load shifting in a dynamic tariff bound residential customer is analysed for single day. After load shifting, energy bill gain of 23.46% without compromising consumer comfort and MD limitation is obtained. It is identified that RTP with load shifting is economic to other schemes however, penalty from MD charges is avoided with a slight variation in energy pricing. Hence, active participation of consumers can be anticipated with dynamic pricing. Switching control of appliances based on tariff schemes can be automated with the help of IoTs based technologies. Hence, optimal ON OFF states of appliances are available for easy hardware implementation. It can be concluded that, the inevitable dynamic pricing can be economised by shifting of appliance loads. Hence, this paper highlights dynamic tariff and energy economy, complex MILP problem is solved without compromising consumer comfort, utility MD limitation and bringing economic benefit to residential consumer. Hence in near future, SMs are anticipated to have such functionalities, to make consumers aware of load shifting benefits, under smart grid paradigm.

References

1. GAMS - The Solver Manuals. GAMS Development Corporation, Washington DC (2001). https://www.gams.com/
2. Aggarwal, A.K., Syed, A.A., Garg, S.: Diffusion of residential RT solar – is lack of funds the real issue? Int. J. Energy Sector Manage. **14**(2), 316–334 (2019). https://doi.org/10.1108/IJESM-2019-0004, https://www.emerald.com/insight/content/doi/10.1108/IJESM-02-2019-0004/full/html
3. Al-Turjman, F., Abujubbeh, M.: IoT-enabled smart grid via SM: an overview. Future Gener. Comput. Syst. **96**, 579–590 (2019). https://doi.org/10.1016/j.future.2019.02.012, https://www.sciencedirect.com/science/article/pii/S0167739X1831759X
4. Alharbi, W., Bhattacharya, K.: Demand response and energy storage in MV islanded microgrids for high penetration of renewables. In: 2013 IEEE Electrical Power & Energy Conference, pp. 1–6. IEEE, Halifax (2013). https://doi.org/10.1109/EPEC.2013.6802928, http://ieeexplore.ieee.org/document/6802928/
5. Anand, H.: A feasibility study on smart residential community for future smart grid in India. IUP J. Electr. Electron. Eng. **10**(2) (2017)
6. Anand, H., Ramasubbu, R.: A real time pricing strategy for remote micro-grid with economic emission dispatch and stochastic renewable energy sources. Renew. Energy **127**, 779–789 (2018)
7. Aslam, S., Javaid, N., Asif, M., Iqbal, U., Iqbal, Z., Sarwar, M.A.: A mixed integer linear programming based optimal home energy management scheme considering grid-connected microgrids. In: 2018 14th International Wireless Communications & Mobile Computing Conference (IWCMC), pp. 993–998. IEEE, Limassol (2018). https://doi.org/10.1109/IWCMC.2018.8450462, https://ieeexplore.ieee.org/document/8450462/
8. Azar, A.G., Jacobsen, R.H.: Appliance Scheduling Optimization for Demand Response. Int. J. Adv. Intell. Syst. **15** (2016)
9. Balakumar, P., Sathiya, S.: Demand side management in smart grid using load shifting technique. In: 2017 IEEE International Conference on Electrical, Instrumentation and Communication Engineering (ICEICE), pp. 1– 6. IEEE, Karur (2017). https://doi.org/10.1109/ICEICE.2017.8191856, http://ieeexplore.ieee.org/document/8191856/

10. Chen, Z., Wu, L., Fu, Y.: Real-time price-based demand response management for residential appliances via stochastic optimization and robust optimization. IEEE Trans. Smart Grid 3(4), 1822–1831 (2012). https://doi.org/10.1109/TSG.2012.2212729, http://ieeexplore.ieee.org/document/6311454/

11. Dai, R., Mesbahi, M.: Optimal power generation and load management for off-grid hybrid power systems with renewable sources via mixed-integer programming. Energy Convers. Manage. 73, 234–244 (2013). https://doi.org/10.1016/j.enconman.2013.04.039, https://linkinghub.elsevier.com/retrieve/pii/S0196890413002367

12. Emami Javanmard, M., Ghaderi, S., Sangari, M.S.: Integrating energy and water optimization in buildings using multi-objective mixed-integer linear programming. Sustainable Cities and Society 62, 102409 (2020). https://doi.org/10.1016/j.scs.2020.102409, https://linkinghub.elsevier.com/retrieve/pii/S2210670720306302

13. Erdinc, O., Paterakis, N.G., Mendes, T.D.P., Bakirtzis, A.G., Catalao, J. P.S.: Smart household operation considering bi-directional EV and ESS utilization by real-time pricing-based DR. IEEE Trans. Smart Grid 6(3), 1281–1291 (2015). https://doi.org/10.1109/TSG.2014.2352650, http://ieeexplore.ieee.org/document/6901266/

14. Gautam, K., Purkayastha, D.: The future of distributed renewable energy in India. In: 2021 Climate Policy Initiative, pp. 1–34 (2021). https://www.climatepolicyinitiative.org/publication/the-future-of-distributed-renewable-energy-in-india/

15. Hammou Ou Ali, I., Ouassaid, M., Maaroufi, M.: Dynamic time and load-based preference toward optimal appliance scheduling in a smart home. Math. Probl. Eng. 2021, 1–16 (2021). https://doi.org/10.1155/2021/6640521, https://www.hindawi.com/journals/mpe/2021/6640521/

16. Wu, H., Pratt, A., Chakraborty, S.: Stochastic optimal scheduling of residential appliances with renewable energy sources. In: 2015 IEEE Power & Energy Society General Meeting, pp. 1–5. IEEE, Denver (2015). https://doi.org/10.1109/PESGM.2015.7286584, http://ieeexplore.ieee.org/document/7286584/

17. Izmitligil, H., Ozkan, H.A.: A home power management system using mixed integer linear programming for scheduling appliances and power resources. In: 2016 IEEE PES Innovative Smart Grid Technologies Conference Europe (ISGT-Europe), pp. 1–6. IEEE, Ljubljana (2016). https://doi.org/10.1109/ISGTEurope.2016.7856241, http://ieeexplore.ieee.org/document/7856241/

18. Kakran, S., Chanana, S.: Energy scheduling of residential community equipped with smart appliances and rooftop solar. In: 2017 7th International Conference on Power Systems (ICPS), pp. 323–327. IEEE, Pune (2017). https://doi.org/10.1109/ICPES.2017.8387314, https://ieeexplore.ieee.org/document/8387314/

19. Kappagantu, R., Daniel, S.A., Suresh, N.: Techno-economic analysis of smart grid pilot project Puducherry. Resour.-Efficient Technol. 2(4), 185–198 (2016). https://doi.org/10.1016/j.reffit.2016.10.001, http://linkinghub.elsevier.com/retrieve/pii/S2405653716301634

20. Luna, A.C., Diaz, N.L., Graells, M., Vasquez, J.C., Guerrero, J.M.: Mixed-integer-linear-programming-based energy management system for hybrid pv-wind-battery microgrids: modeling, design, and experimental verification. IEEE Trans. Power Electron. 32(4), 2769–2783 (2017). https://doi.org/10.1109/TPEL.2016.2581021, http://ieeexplore.ieee.org/document/7492611/

21. Paridari, K., Parisio, A., Sandberg, H., Johansson, K.H.: Energy and CO2 efficient scheduling of smart appliances in active houses equipped with batteries. In: 2014 IEEE International Conference on Automation Science and Engineering (CASE), pp. 632–639. IEEE, Taipei (2014). https://doi.org/10.1109/CoASE.2014.6899394, http://ieeexplore.ieee.org/document/6899394/

22. Pradhan, J.K., Verma, P.P., Khemka, V., Anoop, V., Srinivas, S., Swarup, K.: Uncertainty handling for Electric Vehicle aggregator using IGDT. In: 2018 20th National Power Systems Conference (NPSC), pp. 1–6. IEEE, Tiruchirappalli (2018). https://doi.org/10.1109/NPSC. 2018.8771745, https://ieeexplore.ieee.org/document/8771745/

23. Qayyum, F.A., Naeem, M., Khwaja, A.S., Anpalagan, A., Guan, L., Venkatesh, B.: Appliance scheduling optimization in smart home networks. IEEE Access 3, 2176–2190 (2015). https:// doi.org/10.1109/ACCESS.2015.2496117, http://ieeexplore.ieee.org/document/7312407/

24. Risbeck, M.J., Maravelias, C.T., Rawlings, J.B., Turney, R.D.: A mixed-integer linear programming model for real-time cost optimization of building heating, ventilation, and air conditioning equipment. Energy Build. 142, 220–235 (2017). https://doi.org/10.1016/j.enb uild.2017.02.053, https://linkinghub.elsevier.com/retrieve/pii/S0378778817306473

25. Sedhom, B.E., El-Saadawi, M.M., El Moursi, M., Hassan, M., Eladl, A.A.: IoT-based optimal demand side management and control scheme for smart microgrid. Int. J. Electr. Power Energy Syst. 127, 106–674 (2021). https://doi.org/10.1016/j.ijepes.2020.106674, https://www.scienc edirect.com/science/article/pii/S0142061520342198

26. Soroudi, A.: Power System Optimization Modeling in GAMS. Springer, Cham (2017). https:// doi.org/10.1007/978-3-319-62350-4

27. Swalehe, H., Marungsri, B.: Intelligent algorithm for optimal load management in smart home appliance scheduling in distribution system. In: 2018 International Electrical Engineering Congress (iEECON), pp. 1–4. IEEE, Krabi (2018). https://doi.org/10.1109/IEECON.2018. 8712166, https://ieeexplore.ieee.org/document/8712166/

Detection of Authorized Nodes to Provide an Optimal Secure Communication in Amalgamated Internet MANET

J. Anitha Josephine[1], S. Senthilkumar[2](✉), R. Rajkumar[3] (iD),
and C. M. Arun Kumar[4] (iD)

[1] Department of AIML, School of Engineering, Malla Reddy University, Hyderabad, India
[2] Department of CSE, University College of Engineering, Pattukkottai, India
senthilucepkt@gmail.com
[3] DSBS, SRM Institute of Science and Technology, Chennai, India
[4] Department of ECE, University College of Engineering, Pattukkottai, India

Abstract. The most required objective in MANET is to identify whether the messages based on routing is established by the authorized node. To solve this issue, the existing systems provided a route among the authorization nodes within the particular environment. The description of the authorization based on the soft security methodology to remove the problems related to security also mentioned in the existing systems. Each and every node used an authorized threshold value. In this regard, our research work proposes an optimal methodology called DTAN (Detecting Authorized nodes) in which authorization components such as integration, Data and social networking are utilized to generate the unique characteristics of authorization in amalgamated MANET. Through these items the proposed work describes the authorization capacity, information integrity and non-static social characteristics of the node. After the detection of authorization nodes, a secure route has been deployed to the outer network by passing the gateway node using the particular secure route attaining value. The proposed approach performs confidential distribution methodology (CDM) to provide a secure communication in MANET. The parameters considered by the proposed system is network performance, packet delivery ratio, routing load and end to end delay. The experimental analysis has been done for both the proposed and existing systems in which the proposed systems increases the performance of the network, reduces the routing load and minimizes the end to end delay when comparing to the existing systems. At the mean time the proposed system ensures a secure data communication in the amalgamated internet MANET.

Keywords: MANET · Authorized nodes · Secure communication · Confidential Distribution · Detecting the Authorized nodes · Packet delivery ratio · End to end delay

1 Introduction

The collection of mobile devices of the wireless network which has been developed for a certain objective by excluding the fixed support is said to be mobile adhoc network

R. Venkataraman et al. (Eds.): ICIoT 2022, CCIS 1727, pp. 93–102, 2023.
https://doi.org/10.1007/978-3-031-28475-5_9

(MANET). The mobile adhoc network will not support the centralized model and linked with the constant networks such as internet or local area network which contains the resources by their own. The connection of constant network with wireless network is said to be amalgamated mobile adhoc network [1]. The important problems in mobile adhoc network are the restricted amount of appliances, lifetime of the battery, wireless network coverage, non-static network topology and security issues. From these sets of items security plays a vital role in MANET [2]. To provide and describing the authorization values among the wireless nodes, the concept authorization is the most needed one [3]. Authorization is based on some of the basic elements such as authorization publishing, authorization update and authorization repudiation [4].

The different characteristics of authorization is mentioned as, the authorization is non-static, the authorization is influenced by some factor, the authorization is non equivalent to the derived parts, the authorization is based on contest and not automatically transitive [5]. The authorization experimental verification includes presence, guidance and understanding of authorization. The experimental verification can be done in both the ways as central experimental verification or distributed experimental verification [6]. Authorization propagation, predictions and combining together are the three main phases of authorization management [7]. The training part of the authorization is calculated by the help of their nearest neighbors and being updated in the authorization table or database [8]. The nearest neighbors will generate "opinions" which is the other side of the authorization and "training" side of authorization is a segment of total sum of authorization [9].

The reason behind the MANET security problem is, the MANET operates is the mode of wireless communication between the mobile nodes and it won't ensure that the presence of the authentication system for the environment. To provide solutions for these types of security issues (like wiretapping, spoofing, and Information snipping) for MANET, many solutions are given by the existing systems through the authorization enabled through web [10]. Some of the solutions for these types of security issues are also provided through the collaboration with an interaction infrastructure. When generally describing, enabling the authorization through web needs various previous relationships, among the nodes to develop the web [11]. In our research work to solve all these type of security issues, the proposed approach called DTAN (Detecting Authorized nodes) along with the mechanism called Confidential Distribution Methodology (CDM) has been introduced. The proposed system works well and produces optimal solutions for the parameters such as network performance, packet delivery ratio, routing load, and end to end delay while compare with the existing systems.

This paper is structured through other various sections such as Sect. 2 deals with the related works for the current area of research in MANETs and security issues in MANETS, Sect. 3 deals with the proposed approach DTAN and CDM and their working procedure through algorithms and architecture sketch, Sect. 4 deals with outcomes which comprises the performance comparison of both the proposed and existing approaches, Sect. 5 deals with the conclusion of this research work.

2 Related Work

This Research work deals with the relevant works carried out during this research work. To maintain the solutions for authorization, three authorization components are used as major parameters in the MANET which is focusses on the threshold. These parameters are suggested by the existing system Composite trust based public key management [12]. This section deals with the related works carried out during this research work. To maintain the solutions for authorization, three authorization components are used as major parameters in the MANET which is focusses on the threshold. These parameters are suggested by the existing system Composite trust based public key management [12]. Many existing systems provided the solutions to solve the security problems in the MANET [14].

The users create the private keys and public keys by their own using this approach. These collection of nodes are permitted to provide authorization relation by issuing the authorization card among themselves by their own methodology [15]. By using the public key infrastructure model, nodes collaborate with infrastructures mentioned for communicating local area networks, public wireless LANs, networks based on cellular, etc. [16]. In general, it's essential to consider the risk posed by natural disasters, which damages the infrastructure of the network [17]. The security characteristics which are all related to the heterogeneous wireless network are described and provided a tool to display the effects of attacks against the multiple and single hop wireless network. These attacks in future will be changed as dangerous attacks against the heterogeneous wireless networks [18].

One of the existing approach used Chinese remainder theorem for protecting the data from illegal access. Here the performance of Chinese remainder theorem was compared with other existing systems and evaluating the result has been done [19]. The selection of the trust node was proposed to enhance the security in MANET whereas the trust nodes are involved in the key generation process [20]. The fellowship model was proposed to control the flooding and packet drop attacks in MANET by punishing the malevolent nodes [21]. Identity based encryption was proposed to enhance the privacy protection and to produce a secure communication in vehicular ad-hoc network [22].

To remove the security related occurrence in the network, each and every node of the network utilizes the authorization threshold value which has been associated with the authorization values. The major three authorization elements are capacity, integrity and social communication are used to calculate the authorization values in the MANET. To remove the security related occurrence in the network, each and every node of the network utilizes the authorization threshold value which has been associated with the authorization values. The major three authorization elements are capacity, integrity and social communication are used to calculate the authorization values in the MANET.

3 Proposed Work

The attainment of the authorization among the nodes are considered as the major security issues in the MANET. The authorization maintenance is described as Publishing, updating, or repudiation of authorization among the nodes. It is necessary to calculate the authorization values of the node in order to process the static networks such as local area network to recruit the components or resources provided by them. The communication link of the static network with MANET is mentioned as communication Link MANET. So in order to identify the authorization nodes which performs the message passing from to and fro in the MANET it is necessary to calculate the authorization values of the nodes.

The sender node is highly concerned to invent a protected gateway to provide security for the node linked to the non-wireless network which transfers someone message through the nearest nodes up to reaching the gateway. The sender node receives more than one response and begins processing the protected route picking values (PRPV) to pick the secure route with maximum route. The novel system is proposed named Detecting the Authorized Nodes (DTAN) which describes the three authorization components such as authorization capacity, information integrity and non-static social characteristics of the node generates the authorization among the nodes.

3.1 Calculation of Authorization Value

Authorization capacity or ability ($A^{\frac{C}{A}}$) describes the ability of node to process the request to calculated as the ratio of packets withdrawn to packets transmitted by the nodes.

$$A^{\frac{C}{A}} = \frac{Total\ Number\ of\ Packets\ withdrawn\ by\ the\ node}{Total\ Number\ of\ Packets\ Transmitted\ by\ the\ node} \tag{1}$$

The authorization information integrity (A^{II}) describes the honesty behavior of the node in attack department calculated using the methodology of cyclic redundancy check described as the information integrity to verify whether the received information is the legal information transmitted by the source.

$$A^{II} = CRC\ estimated\ for\ information\ transmitted$$
$$= CRC\ estimated\ for\ received\ information \tag{2}$$

$$A^{SC} = \frac{Total\ Count\ of\ Nodes\ Trained}{Sum\ of\ number\ of\ nodes\ in\ the\ environment} \tag{3}$$

The Authorization values depending upon these three elements are calculated and verified and correlated with an authorization value to detect the authorized nodes. The proposed DTAN's architecture and operational model are depicted in Fig. 1.

$$PRPV = A^{\frac{C}{A}} + Ability\ of\ Load + Sum\ of\ Hops \tag{4}$$

where, (A^{II}) is authorization information integrity, (A^{SC}) is Authorization Social Characteristics.

3.2 Proposed Algorithm - Detecting the Authorized Nodes to Attain PRPV

Step 1: The combination of both wired and wireless network has been developed for the mobile nodes and initiate the procedure for developing the gateway.

Step 2: The node sends a Gateway-Someone message GW-SOM to the nearest nodes. The GW-SOL contains the information such as request from the destination or receiver (R_{Req}), address of the source node or the sender node (SN_{Addr}), key of the source node or the sender node (SN_K), address of the gateway (GW_{Addr}), number of nodes (n) and authorization (a) and inverse key or decryption key of the source node (SN_K^{-1}).

Step 3: if the nearest one is a gateway and there is a route for the gateway already present in the environment, then computation process starts to identify the authorization values based on these three authorization components $(A^{\frac{C}{A}}, A^{II}, A^{SC})$, otherwise if the nearest one is not the gateway and there is a route for the gateway already present in the environment, then again publish the GW-SOM information to next nearest node until the node reaches the gateway.

Step 4: The authorization values are calculated using the authorization elements after receiving the GW-SOM information on the gateway receiver side. Now the gateway responds with the Gateway – publication message GW-PBM. The GW-PBM contains information such as response from the destination or receiver (R_{Res}), address of the source node or the sender node (SN_{Addr}), identity of the gateway ID_{GW}, the secure gateway publication message (GW-PBM)SN-GW$_{Source}$, number of nodes (N), authorization (a) and inverse key or decryption key of the source node (GW_K^{-1}).

Step 5: The GW-PBM message is generated with the timestamp by the gateway and by using the distributed secret key encryption is performed.

Step 6: The calculation of authorization values, ability of load and hops count are performed for each and every in between node from gateway to sender node or source node.

Step 7: Transmit the publication message GW-PBM to the nearest node.

Step 8: if Authorization value (AV) greater than or equal to $\geq$ authorization threshold (AT) then process the same step 6, else if authorization value less than $<$ authorization threshold, then such node is said to be the malevolent node.

Step 9: The source or sender node receives decrypted message of GW-PBM with the distributed shared key and computes the values of PRPV and attains the route which has the maximum value of PRPV.

Step 10: The source or sender node generates the request for registration and these requests are checked by the gateway on the receiver side and responses via the route that has been published.

Step 11: Lastly, the source or sender node is linked to the static network and registered with the gateway.

3.3 Proposed Confidential Distribution Methodology (CDN)

Confidential distribution methodology is a technique in which a distributor allocates the shares to the nodes in which only the authorized collection of nodes will be allowed reframe the confidential information. For an instant of confidential distribution methodology is the (M, p) threshold approach. In this approach, a user who produces a confidential divide it in to p shares and allocates each and every shares to the p members preset in the group. The confidential information can be reframed if anyone of the members present in the group collects M shares among the p members. This (M, p) threshold approach can be considered for the wired environment to ensure the security in the wired communication. In cases such as, when a sender is willing to share a confidential information with the receiver node, the sender node will produce variety of shares by using the confidential distribution methodology through various communication channel or path. At the same time, the chance of gathering needed shares in the wired environment may be minimum. So it becomes complex to encrypt an information to be transferred in the MANET. Because the information shared can be sniffed easily and the confidential data can be retrieved by the malevolent node. In order to protect nodes rather than the legal nodes from sniffing the secret information it should be done with extra care which is mentioned in Fig. 2 procedure below.

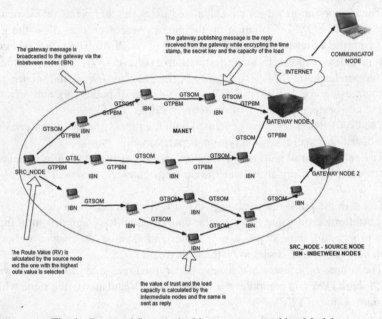

Fig. 1. Proposed System Architecture cum working Model.

4   Results and Discussions

The results are obtained and evaluated using the simulation called network simulator version 2. The parameters used for the result comparison of both existing and proposed approach is end-to-end delay, network performance, packet-delivery ratio, and normalized routing load. The performance of the existing approaches such as WLBAODV, CTPKM and ITWN are evaluated and compared with the proposed approach detecting the Authorized nodes (DTAN) which includes the proposed operational approach based on security is CDM confidential distributional methodology.

The Fig. 3 depicts the performance comparison of both the existing systems and proposed system regarding the packet delivery ratio (Table 1).

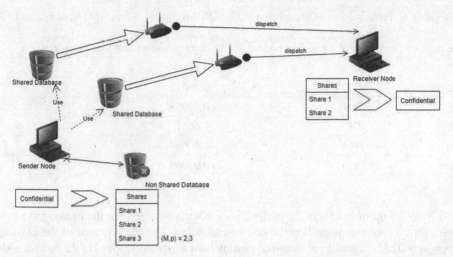

Fig. 2. Secure Communication Methodology using (M.p) threshold approach.

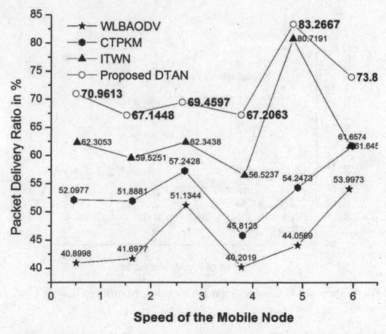

Fig. 3. Proposed vs Existing Approach regarding Packet Delivery Ratio.

Figure 4 depicts the performance comparison of both the existing systems and proposed system regarding the normalized routing load. The performance of the existing approach CTPKM regarding normalized routing load whereas the speed of the mobile node varies from 0.58413 to 5.92985 and the normalized routing load varies from 0.80689

Table 1. Performances of the existing WLBAODV regarding Normalized Routing Load

S. no	Speed of the mobile node	Normalized routing load in packets
1	0.55478	0.59668
2	1.68437	0.76013
3	2.66901	0.76953
4	3.8174	1.6011
5	4.87864	1.00054
6	5.97835	0.93469

to 0.87698. Figure 5 depicts the performance comparison of both the existing systems and proposed system regarding the end-to-end delay. The performance of the existing approach DTAN regarding normalized routing load whereas the speed of the mobile node varies from 0.51762 to 5.95756 and the normalized routing load varies from 0.25059 to 0.51074.

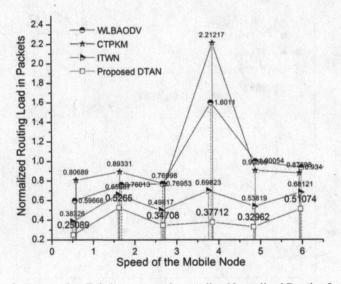

Fig. 4. Proposed vs Existing Approach regarding Normalized Routing Load.

The Fig. 5 depicts the performance comparison of both the existing systems and proposed system regarding the end to end delay. The performance of the existing approach WLBAODV regarding End to End delay and the speed of the mobile node varies from 0.52381 to 6 and the end-to-end delay varies from 0.37241 to 0.88552.

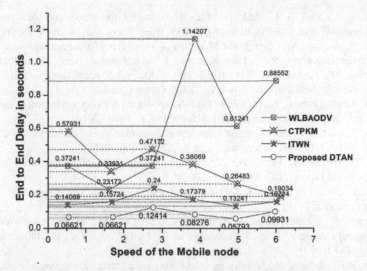

Fig. 5. Proposed vs Existing Approach regarding End to End Delay.

5   Conclusion

Due to minimum bandwidth, distributed operations and utilization of dynamic topologies in MANET various security-related problems are having maximum chance of their occurrence in the MANET environment. Authorization is an approach that will occur in many different types of applications, which are the starting point for the dividing in terminology of authorization maintenance. Many techniques are suggested to describe the authorization maintenance in MANET at the same time none of the techniques described the authorization maintenance methodology in amalgamated internet MANET. So the authorization maintenance is one of the main thing in MANET which has been described by the amalgamated internet MANET through the proposed approach. The results of the proposed approach is evaluated and compared with existing methodologies.

References

1. Khan, K.U.R., Zaman, R.U., Venugopal Reddy, A.: Integrating mobile ad hoc networks and the internet: challenges and a review of strategies. In: 3rd International Conference on Communication Systems Software and Middleware and Workshops, COMSWARE 2008, 6–10 January, (IEEE CNF) pp. 536–543 (2008)
2. Xie, B., Kumar, A.: A framework for internet and ad hoc network security. In: IEEE Symposium on Computers and Communications (ISCC), June (2004)
3. Manoharan, R., Mohanalakshmie, S.: A trust based gateway selection scheme for integration of MANET with Internet. In: IEEE-International Conference on Recent Trends in Information Technology, ICRTIT 2011 MIT, Anna University, Chennai, 3–5 June (2011)
4. Vijayan, R., Jeyanthi, N.: A survey of trust management in mobile ad hoc networks. IEEE Xplore (2016)
5. Virendra, M., Jadliwala, M., Chandrasekaran, M., Upadhyaya, S.: Quantifying trust in mobile ad-hoc networks. IEEE Xplore (2005)

6. Chang, B.-J., Kuo, S.-L.: Markov chain trust model for trust-value analysis and key management in distributed multicast MANETs. IEEE Trans. Veh. Technol. **58**(5) (2009)
7. Cho, J.-H., Swami, A., Chen, I.-R.: Modeling and analysis of trust management with trust chain optimization in mobile ad hoc networks. J. Netw. Comput. Appl. **35**(3) (2010)
8. Anugraha, M., Krishnaveni, S.H.: IEEE Xplore document-recent survey on efficient trust management in mobile ad hoc networks. IEEE Xplore (2016)
9. Douss, A.B.C., Abassi, R., Fatmi, S.G.E.: A trust-based security environment in MANET: definition and performance evaluation. Science Direct, Paris (2016)
10. Hamouid, K., Adi, K.: Efficient certificateless web-of-trust model for public-key authentication in MANET. Comput. Commun. Arch. **63**(C), 24–39 (2015)
11. Kudo, T., Yokota, H., Idoue, A.: A proposal of secure ad hoc routing protocol with an infrastructural support, CQ, RCS2005 (2005)
12. Cho, J.H., Chen, I.-R., Chan, K.S.: Trust threshold based public key management in mobile ad hoc networks (2016)
13. Kobayashi, K., Totani, Y., Utsu, K., Ishii, H.: Achieving secure communication over MANET using secret sharing schemes. J. Supercomput. **72**(3), 1215–1225 (2016). https://doi.org/10.1007/s11227-016-1657-3
14. Zaman, R.U., Sultana, R.: Identifying trustworthy nodes in an integrated Internet MANET to establish a secure communication. In: Bhateja, V., Tavares, J.M.R.S., Rani, B.P., Prasad, V.K., Raju, K.S. (eds.) Proceedings of the Second International Conference on Computational Intelligence and Informatics. AISC, vol. 712, pp. 321–328. Springer, Singapore (2018). https://doi.org/10.1007/978-981-10-8228-3_29
15. Cho, J.H., Chen, I.-R., Chan, K.S.: A survey on trust management for mobile ad hoc networks (2016)
16. Hamidian, A.: A study of internet connectivity for mobile ad hoc networks in NS2. Master's thesis, Department of Communication Systems, Lund Institute of Technology, Lund University (2003)
17. Kowsigan, M., Balasubramanie, P.: A novel resource clustering model to develop an efficient wireless personal cloud environment. Turk. J. Electr. Eng. Comput. Sci. **27**(3), 2156–2169 (2018)
18. Xie, B., Kumar, A., Zhao, D., Reddy, R., He, B.: On secure communication in integrated heterogeneous wireless networks. Int. J. Inf. Technol. Commun. Convergence (IJITCC) **1**(1) (2010)
19. Sinha, D., Bhattacharya, U., Chaki, R.: A CRT based encryption methodology for secure communication in MANET. Int. J. Comput. Appl. **39**(16) (2012)
20. Jenitha, T., Jayashree, P.: Distributed trust node selection for secure group communication in MANET. In: 2014 Fourth International Conference on Advances in Computing and Communications, Cochin, pp. 179–182 (2014)
21. Balakrishnan, V., Varadharajan, V., Tupakula, U.K.: Fellowship: defense against flooding and packet drop attacks in MANET. In: 2006 IEEE/IFIP Network Operations and Management Symposium NOMS 2006, Vancouver, BC, pp. 1–4 (2006)
22. Hwang, R.J., Hsiao, Y., Liu, Y.: Secure communication scheme of VANET with privacy preserving. In: 2011 IEEE 17th International Conference on Parallel and Distributed Systems, Tainan, pp. 654–659 (2011)

Enhanced Hybrid Optimization Technique to Find Optimal Solutions for Task Scheduling in Cloud-Fog Computing Environments

Anjali Patle[✉], Sai Dheeraj Kanaparthi, and K. Jairam Naik

Department of CSE, National Institute of Technology Raipur, Raipur 492001, Chhattisgarh, India
anjalipatle1417@gmail.com, kanaparthi.saidheeraj@gmail.com,
Jnaik.cse@nitrr.ac.in

Abstract. Fog-node computing, in culmination with computing using cloud-network environment, has emerged as a promising improvement for Internet of Things (IoT) architectures. Computing using fog-nodes is a decentralized concept which includes the distribution of various resources like the processing power, storage capacity, and applications between the central cloud structure and the source of data. Fog nodes provide the benefits and power of the cloud nodes, closer to the point of data creation and consumption. Hence this architecture provides a flexible and efficient system for handling IoT tasks as per their resource requirements. We propose a hybrid optimization technique which combines the Optimization Algorithm based on Artificial Ecosystem (AEO) as well as the widely popular Algorithm based on Salp-Swarm together to improve the exploitation abilities of AEO. A system model is also described which shows various layers in the cloud-fog environment for IoT systems. These layers interact together to create an efficient architecture where optimization techniques can be applied to develop optimal task scheduling.

The developed hybrid algorithm is simulated using a synthetic dataset consisting of various non-preemptive tasks with each task length between 1–200000 MI. Its performance is analyzed by the use of metrics like makespan time and Performance Improvement Ratio, which shows an improvement of a maximum of 2.2% when compared with existing AEO algorithm. Finally, the scope for future development of this algorithm and this field is also discussed. The algorithm was implemented and analyzed using Java SDK-1.7 and MATLAB R2021b software.

Keywords: Task Scheduling · Artificial Ecosystem Optimization · Salp-Swarm

1 Introduction

1.1 Overview

With advancement in information technology and continuously improving availability of technology and hardware at lower costs, Internet of Things (*IoT*) has become a prominent field in the technological world. Now, billions of devices at every scale are connected

© The Author(s), under exclusive license to Springer Nature Switzerland AG 2023
R. Venkataraman et al. (Eds.): ICIoT 2022, CCIS 1727, pp. 103–114, 2023.
https://doi.org/10.1007/978-3-031-28475-5_10

to the internet for sharing, collecting and analyzing information through IoT [1]. These devices can connect to a network and collect data intelligently through the use of sensors and monitors, which can then be shared in real-time for various applications, all without any need for human intervention.

With such enormous amount of data being generated from various devices in the IoT systems, efficient storing and processing this data is a crucial aspect. Cloud computing provides an excellent platform to enable the various components of the IoT to access compute resources and storage capacity facilities at a huge centralized level. A number of resources and services can be pooled in the cloud computing system to provide numerous functionalities to the devices connected in the IoT system. However, one drawback of the cloud computing services is the lack of efficiency in dealing with data generated in real-time. Therefore, nowadays Fog-Computing is extensively used in conjunction with cloud computing to provide the ability of effective real-time communication.

It is important to note that the fog computing systems do not aim at replacing the cloud computing infrastructure. Instead, they work complementarily by dividing the IoT tasks based on various parameters. Fog nodes are relatively smaller-scale systems that can enable faster short-term analytics of generated data for time-critical processes. These can save time when IoT devices are dealing with tasks that require instantaneous responses [2]. On the other hand, cloud nodes are powerful and robust platforms that can perform resource-intensive processes such as tasks based on machine-learning and advanced analytics, which can consume more time for communication with the cloud servers. Therefore, cloud and fog computing form an efficient architecture for IoT systems, providing functionalities for varied requirements. A typical cloud and fog computing environment for IoT systems is described in Fig. 1.

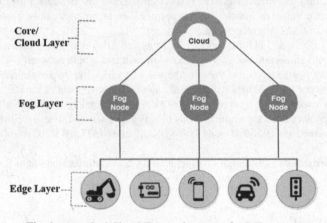

Fig. 1. A typical Cloud-Fog environment for IoT systems

The primary advantage of fog computing is the reduction in the time required for a response and system's latency. The transfer of data from devices situated towards the network-edge, to the central cloud computing unit can consume a lot of time. This data can be processed in the fog nodes near the end-devices, which can provide near real-time responsiveness in the system. It can also help in minimizing the bandwidth of the network and the cost associated with it by reducing the data amount which is required to be transferred to the cloud. It is also network-agnostic and can be developed over wired, 5 G or Wi-Fi based networks with flexibility. However, there exist certain startup cost for hardware that should be factored in while deciding the degree of fog-computing that should be introduced in the network. Fog-nodes are distributed geographically, which works in contrast with the centralized nature of cloud-computing, where any connected component can utilize the cloud's resources from any location and at any instant. Therefore, a careful balance is required to efficiently used cloud architectures in combination with the fog environment for IoT.

The paper is arranged as follows. Sect. 2 contains related work to the main topic. Sect. 3 and 4 contain background on the two algorithms, Artificial Ecosystem-based Optimization (AEO), and Salp-Swarm Algorithm (AEOSSA) respectively. In Sect. 5, the proposed hybrid algorithm AEOSSA is explained. We've described the experimental setup and evaluation metrics in Sect. 6 and finally conclude in Sect. 7.

1.2 Objectives

a. The primary intent of this project is to combine the benefits of the existing algorithms, namely Optimization algorithm based on Artificial Ecosystem and the Algorithm based on Salp-Swarm, in order to create a hybrid optimization technique that can remedy the drawbacks faced when the existing AEO algorithm is used.
b. Describe a system model and its various layers that can be used to apply such algorithms for optimization in order to improve scheduling of tasks in cloud-fog-node IoT environments.

The intent of improving efficiency and mitigating the system latency in IoT frameworks is of great importance due to the time-critical nature of various processes carried out in IoT systems. Reducing the response time for the generated tasks requests can help in yielding the benefits of fog-computing in an efficient manner, where the presence of fog nodes can be utilized effectively.

2 Related Work

The time complexity for scheduling multi-task systems is considered to be NP-Hard. Therefore, many intelligent techniques and algorithms for optimization have been proposed in literature. Nyugen et al. considered the balance between task arrangements and time-cost and proposed an evolutionary algorithm [3] that can enhance the scheduling of tasks in environments of cloud nodes and fog nodes. Boveiri et al. proposed an improvement over the ant colony optimization algorithm for multiprocessor environments [4]. This improvement is applied to create a task scheduling approach that optimizes the order of task execution. Tong et al. combined the power of Q-leaning algorithm with neural network to formulated a new artificial intelligence algorithm called Q-leaning TS [5], which is proposed to efficiently handle task scheduling architectures containing cloud systems for computing. Game strategy was used by Yang et al. to enhance the solidity behind tasks in IoT systems that are executed in an environment containing cloud nodes

[6]. Yang et al. introduced an evolutionary technique that works on multiple objectives for efficient task organizing in computing systems of fog nodes [7]. This method primarily aimed at enhancing the technique for allocation of resources and time involved in performance.

Mtshali et al. used a visualization method that aimed at determining the proper cost of energy while maintaining a low time consumption in computing systems with fog nodes [8]. This algorithm used K Means based on resource clustering. Zeng et al. worked on developing a task scheduling algorithm for embedded systems present in fog-computing environments. This technique focused on minimizing the task execution duration while managing the user activity [9].

Zhao et al. proposed the Optimization algorithm based on Artificial Ecosystem which a metaheuristic technique evolved by observing the behavior of organisms in nature [10]. It is developed by considering the energy-course among various creatures present inside a system of organisms. The organisms under consideration are namely herbivores, carnivores and omnivores. This algorithm simulates three processes of the ecosystem in a mathematical construct. These processes are producing of energy, consuming energy and decomposing organisms. The technique has been employed proficiently for resolving numerous problems for optimizing parameters, which includes engineering problems, tuberculosis diagnosis, tuning PID controllers in AVR systems, parameter identification and extraction, etc.

Algorithm based on Salp-Swarm has been suggested by Mir Jalili et al. to address various engineering problems based on the concept of population-based optimization algorithms [11]. It is a metaheuristic technique which was inspired by the behavior of groups or swarms of Salps that navigate and forage through the ocean together. This method was previously utilized to numerous artificial intelligence applications, including selection of feature, big data optimization and image segmentation. It has also been used to estimate the parameters of photovoltaic models (PV) and parameters of power system stabilizers, as well as some engineering problems. Salp-Swarm algorithm was also applied to predict chemical activities as in. Various improvements over these existing algorithms have also been suggesting. Tubhishat et al. proposed an upgraded version of the algorithm based on Salp-Swarm using learning techniques on opposition concept and algorithm of local search. This method was created for selection of features based on the algorithms of locally-based search to minimize the problem of locally-obtained optimal values.

Also, there are several approaches proposed by K J Naik & K Jairam Naik et al. [13–17] for the task distribution, load balancing and VM live migration and suggested optimal solutions for task scheduling in cloud-fog computing environments. These approaches perform better under low to high workload conditions. The workflow management approaches and the fog node recommendation methods suggested by them is a well considerable approaches in the dynamic cloud-fog environment. The benefits of these individual approaches can be unified for the betterment of a multitenant complex clod-fog environments.

The exploitation abilities of the AEO algorithm can be improved to produce better results and the proposed algorithm aims at solving this gap. The Salp-swarm algorithm has been applied for various engineering problems, but it's application in cloud computing is a good ground for development. Artificial Ecosystem based Optimization algorithm can be developed for addressing Task Scheduling problem as well. The proposed algorithm covers these gaps by developing a hybrid methodology.

3 Artificial Ecosystem Optimization (AEO)

An ecosystem is described as the combination of living organisms, their physical environment and their interrelationships in a particular space. The concept of "Ecosystem" was brought by A.G. Tansley in 1955 [10] and is divided into two: Non-living elements like air, water, etc. and living refer to the living organisms. These are bifurcated into producer, consumer and decomposer. The flow of nutrients from the producers to decomposers is important in the ecosystem.

Producers are those who generally are providers of food. Most of them are green plants that get their food from photosynthesis. Consumers are those who cannot make their own food and hence consume from other sources such as plants (herbivores), other animals/meat (carnivores), or both (omnivores). Decomposers refers to fungi that feed themselves organisms' dead matter, and converts them into water, minerals and carbon dioxide. The products of Decomposers are then used by plants which through photosynthesis generates oxygen and sugar, coming to the end of cycle. A food chain describes where each entity gets their food from, to achieve the nutrients flow in the ecosystem. This is where producers, consumers interact with each other.

In AEO, there are three operators [10] i.e. consumption, decomposition, production. The Production operator improves the stability between exploration and exploitation. The Consumption operator is used to better the exploration. The third operator, it is made to increase the exploitation.

Exploration refers to finding of an optimum solution of the problem, whereas Exploitation refers to the repeated use of the optimum solution until exhaustion.

AEO follows certain rules [12]: The population (ecosystem) contains producers, consumers and decomposers. Only one producer and decomposer exist in the population. Remaining are consumers, with equal probabilities of herbivores, carnivores and omnivores. The energy level is computed by a function that computes a fitness value and is arranged in the decreasing order so that high fitness values correspond to high energy levels for a minimization problem.

To summarize, in AEO, as the name suggests, there is an ecosystem in place where producers, consumers and decomposers exist. Some of them act as food for another, thus there is flow of nutrients, thus comprising a chain from producers to decomposers and vice-versa. The exploration of food sources and exploitation is described using rules and a few mathematical models thus making it useful to solve Task Scheduling problems.

4 Salp Swarm Algorithm

Salp Swarm originates from oceanic creatures called Salpidae [11]. They're transparent barrel shaped creatures with jellyfish like tissues structure. They roam in deep water in search of food in swarms. When a food is nearby, they form a salp chains. These chains are mathematically formed where there is one leader salp, and the others are all followers. Their behavior enhances when food is nearby. First, the population is initialized considering Ubb (upper bound) and Lbb (lower bound). Then the following statements i.e. computing fitness of each salp, finding follower salps and updating the salp population about the followers is looped until the terminal condition is unmet. Once the control flow is out of the loop, the food source is chosen and then the position is updated of the leader and the follower salps.

5 Proposed Algorithm

The proposed AEOSSA algorithm [12], during its exploration phases, the operators of AEO (Artificial Ecosystem Optimization) are used, and in the exploitation phase at the end, the operators of AEO [10] or SSA [11] (Salp Swarm Algorithm) are used depending on the value of a probability factor as specified further.

5.1 Initial Stage

Here, the solutions of the Task Scheduling problem are represented by fixing the starting value for a group of "N" integer solutions. These are then computed for quality compared by its value of fitness given through objective function.

$$X_{ij} = floor\left(Lbb_{ij} + \propto \times \left(Ubb_{ij} - Lbb_{ij}\right)\right), \propto \in [0, 1], j = 1, 2, \ldots, n \tag{1}$$

5.2 Updating Stage

During the updating stage, solution is enhanced and decided through competition among AEO/SSA operators. The solution with least makespan is marked as an extremely good solution and the others are renewed accordingly. These solutions would be utilized to explore the search area and renew their locations using the AEO operators.

The optimal solutions within the respective regions are renewed by AEO/SSA operators in relation to probability (Pr_i), after which X_{ij} (1) is updated. These steps are looped until the terminal conditions are reached. The fitness value Val_i is used to find the probability.

$$Pr_i = \frac{Val_i}{\sum_{i=1}^{N} Val_i} \tag{2}$$

$$X_{ij} = \begin{cases} AEO \text{ operators } Pr_i > r_a \\ SSA \text{ operators } otherwise \end{cases} \tag{3}$$

$$r_a = \min(Pr_i) + rand \times (\max(Pr_i) - \min(Pr_i)), rand \in [0, 1] \tag{4}$$

The pseudocode for the proposed AEOSSA technique is described in Algorithm (1). This pseudocode shows the various steps that are required to implement the proposed algorithm. It begins with describing the input parameters t_{max}, n and m. Then we begin by initializing the population as integer values for the given cloud-fog environment. For $t = 1$ to $t = t_{max}$ iterations, the loop is repeated in which first the best solution is found by calculating the fitness value. Then this solution is updated for the production phase. Following this, each solution from $I = 2$ to $I = N$ is chosen on a random basis to select an organism as either a carnivore, omnivore or herbivore, and it is updated using the consumption phase Eqs. (2–3). Following this, the best solution is again obtained by fitness values and decomposition is done on this solution using the probability factor introduced in the AEOSSA technique. All the three phases are repeated t_{max} times. Here, VMs list (m), IoT tasks list (n), number of solutions (N), total number of iterations (t_{max}) are initialized with integer population, to calulcate integral solutions (X).

Algorithm 1: Pseudocode of AEOSSA algorithm

1: Input: *(m)*: VMs list, *(n)*: IoT tasks list, *(N)* number of solutions, total number of iterations*(t_{max})*,

2: The integer population is initialized in order to calculate the integral solutions *(X)*.

3: Set the iterating variable $t = 1$.

4: **while** $t <= t_{max}$ **do**

5: For X_i, compute the fitness value (F_i).

6: Determine X_b. which is the best solution

7:         Use Eq. (1-3) to update X_i. This refers to the production phase.

8: **for** $j = 2, 3, ..., N$ **do**

9:     **if** *rand* < 1/3 **then**

10:         X_j is a herbivore

11:         Use Eq. (4) to enhance X_j

12:     **else if** 1/3 < *rand* < 2/3 **then**

13:         X_j is a carnivore

14:         Use Eq. (5) to enhance X_j

15:     **else**

16:         X_j is an omnivore

17:         Use Eq. (6) to enhance X_j

18:     For each X_j, compute the fitness

19:     Update X_b.

20:     Compute the probability of each solution i.e. Pr_i, using Eq. (13) to compute the probability. This factor determines the use of operators in the decomposition phase, i.e. AEO or SSA.

21:     Calculate the value of r_a

22:     **if** $Pr_i > r_s$ **then**

23:         Use operators of AEO

24:     **else**

25:         Use operators of SSA

The flowchart for the developed algorithm is described in Fig. 2. This figure shows the control flow of the whole algorithm, which can be divided into the three phases of production, consumption and decomposition. The flowchart describes how initialization of the solution is followed by production phase, which is followed by consumption phase. It also shows how decomposition phase is carried out using the operators of AEO and SSA.

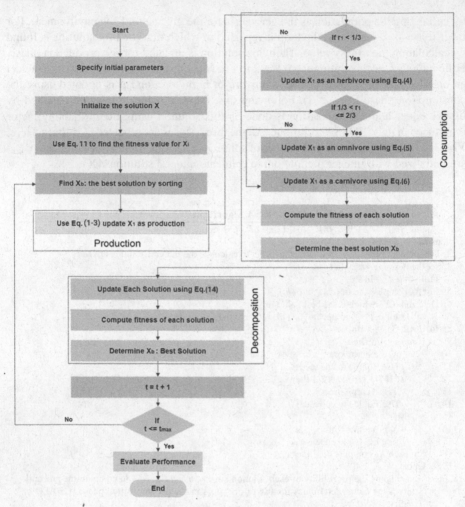

Fig. 2. Flow chart of the developed algorithm AEOSSA.

6 Simulation

The execution and performance analysis of the developed algorithm was conducted using MATLAB R2021b software. The core algorithm was developed using Java and compiled using Java SDK-1.7. The experiments were conducted using a HP PC consisting of an Intel® Core™ i7-7300HQ 2.50 GHz CPU in a 64-bit Windows-10 OS. For carrying out the experiments, the cloud-fog environments can be assumed to be divided among two data centers, 25 virtual machines running on four host machines. The developed algorithm has various parameters and random variables which are used in the equations described earlier. The Parameters specification for experimentation are as provided in the Table 1.

Table 1. Parameters specification for experimentation

Cloud entities	Parameters	Values
Datacenter	Datacenters no	2
Host	Number of hosts	4
	Size of RAM	16 GB
	Type of Policy	Time-Shared
	Bandwidth	10 Gb/s
VM	VMs No	25
	Capacity of CPU	[100–5000] MIPS
	Number of CPUs	1
	Type of policy	Time-Shared
	Bandwidth	1 Gb/s
	RAM Size	1 GB
	Storage	20 GB
Client	Number of Client	[50, 100]

The Salp-Swarm Algorithm operators function by using the swarm size, k1, k2 and k3 values. The swarm size here is same as the population that is used for Artificial Ecosystem-based algorithm. The values of k1, k2 and k3 are used in the exploitation phases and are generated randomly within a range each time. The Artificial Ecosystem-based Algorithm also uses the population size or swarm size parameter. It uses rand1, rand2, rand3 and rand4 parameters in its decomposition, consumption and decomposition phases. Size of population used is same as the one used in Salp-Swarm Algorithm. The developed algorithm is compared with the existing Artificial Ecosystem-based Algorithm. This algorithm will use all the parameters used in both AEO and Salp-Swarm Algorithm. Hence, its parameters include swarm size, rand1, rand2, rand3 and rand4, as well as, k1, k2 and k3. A synthetic dataset was used to carry out these experiments and to analyze the efficacy of the algorithm. This data consisted of various tasks with each task length between 1–200000 MI. These tasks are considered to be non-preemptive and independent from each other.

Taking the Fig. 3 & Fig. 4 into consideration, we see that Salp Swarm Algorithm (SSA) has makespan times ranging from 0.923 s to 0.762 s whereas, the Artificial-Ecosystem based optimization based algorithm has the values ranging from 0.797 s - 0.604 s. AEO performs better than SSA because of the presence of three phases in the AEO technique, in which the first phase of production balances between the exploration and exploitation of the algorithm, thereby helping in searching and enhancing the solution is the search-space. Hence, AEO algorithm gives better results as compared to the Salp-Swarm Algorithm as displayed in Fig. 3 & Fig. 4.

Considering AEO and AEOSSA, the AEOSSA first uses the operators of AEO for exploration, as that is its better ability. Thus both of them have similar values at the

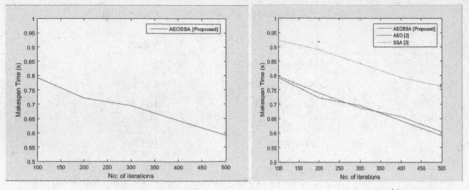

Fig. 3. Makespan time values for AEOSSA with no. of iterations

Fig. 4. Comparison of AEOSSA vs other Algo.

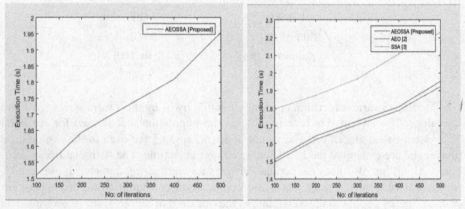

Fig. 5. Execution time of AEOSSA

Fig. 6. Execution time of AEOSSA vs other Algo.

start, ranging from 0.79s to 0.60s. But where it differs is the last value where AEO comes out with 0.604s and AEOSSA comes out with 0.591s. This is because, at the end in AEOSSA, depending on a probability factor, the operator of AEO or SSA is used to improve exploitation. Hence, we see a lower Execution time value in AEOSSA as compared to AEO as displayed in Fig. 5 & Fig. 6.

7 Conclusion

An enhanced hybrid optimization algorithm has been discussed to addressed scheduling task issues in Cloud/Fog computing environments. This is an improvement over the Optimization based on Artificial Ecosystem algorithm, which is a metaheuristic technique inspired by nature. It is based on the flow of energy as observed in the nature and it uses three phases to simulate it. However, this algorithm lacks in its exploitation abilities. Therefore, we use Salp-Swarm algorithm to remedy this shortcoming of AEO algorithm to develop our hybrid optimization technique. The base algorithms of AEO and Salp-Swarm has solved various engineering problems successfully. This algorithm can also be developed further to create its application in fields like vehicle routing and job shop scheduling.

References

1. Ghasempour, A.: Internet of things in smart grid: architecture, applications, services, key technologies, and challenges. Inventions **4**(1), 22 (2019)
2. Vijayalakshmi, R., Vasudevan, V., Kadry, S., Lakshmana Kumar, R.: Optimization of makespan and resource utilization in the fog computing environment through task scheduling algorithm. Int. J. Wavelets Multiresolut. Inform. Process. **18**(01), 1941025 (2020)
3. Nguyen, B.M., Thi Thanh Binh, H., Do Son, B., et al.: Evolutionary algorithms to optimize task scheduling problem for the IoT based bag-of-tasks application in cloud-fog computing environment. Appl. Sci. **9**(9) 1730 (2019)
4. Boveiri, H.R., Khayami, R., Elhoseny, M., Gunasekaran, M.: An efficient swarm-intelligence approach for task scheduling in cloud-based internet of things applications. J. Ambient Intell. Humanized Comput. **10**(9), 3469–3479 (2019)
5. Tong, Z., Chen, H., Deng, X., Li, K., Li, K.: A scheduling scheme in the cloud computing environment using deep Q-learning. Inform. Sci. **512**, 1170–1191 (2020)
6. Yang, X., Rahmani, N.: Task scheduling mechanisms in fog computing: review, trends, and perspectives. Kybernetes (2020)
7. Yang, M., Ma, H., Wei, S., Zeng, Y., Chen, Y., Hu, Y.: A multi-objective task scheduling method for fog computing in cyber-physical-social services. IEEE Access **8**, 65085–65095 (2020)
8. Mtshali, M., Kobo, H., Dlamini, S., Adigun, M., Mudali, P.: Multi-objective optimization approach for task scheduling in fog computing. In: 2019 International Conference on Advances in Big Data, Computing and Data Communication Systems, IcABCD. IEEE, pp. 1–6 (2019)
9. Zeng, D., Gu, L., Guo, S., Cheng, Z., Yu, S.: Joint optimization of task scheduling and image placement in fog computing supported software-defined embedded system. IEEE Trans. Comput. **65**(12), 3702–3712 (2016)
10. Zhao, W., Wang, L., Zhang, Z.: Artificial ecosystem-based optimization: a novel nature-inspired meta-heuristic algorithm. Neural Comput. Appl. **32**(13), 9383–9425 (2019). https://doi.org/10.1007/s00521-019-04452-x
11. Mirjalili, S., Gandomi, A.H., Mirjalili, S.Z., Saremi, S., Faris, H., Mirjalili, S.M.: Salp swarm algorithm: a bio-inspired optimizer for engineering design problems. Adv. Eng. Softw. **114**, 163–191 (2017)
12. Abd Elaziz, M., Abualigah, L., Attiya, I.: Advanced optimization technique for scheduling IoT tasks in cloud-fog computing environments. Future Gener. Comput. Syst. **124**, 142–154 (2021). ISSN 0167–739X
13. Jairam Naik, K.: A cloud-fog computing system for classification and scheduling the information-centric IoT applications. Int. J. Commun. Netw. Distrib. Syst. **27**(4), 388–423 (2021). https://doi.org/10.1504/IJCNDS.2021.10039780
14. Jairam Naik, K.: A deadline based elastic approach for balanced task scheduling in computing cloud environment. Int. J. Cloud Comput. (IJCC) **10**(5/6), 579–602 (2021). https://doi.org/10.1504/IJCC.2021.120396
15. Jairam Naik, K., Pedagandam, M., Mishra, A.: Workflow scheduling optimization for distributed environment using artificial neural networks and reinforcement learning (WfSo_ANRL). Int. J. Comput. Sci. Eng. (IJCSE) **24**(6), 653–670 (2021). https://doi.org/10.1504/IJCSE.2021.10041146

16. Naik, K.J.: A co-scheduling system for fog-node recommendation and load management in cloud-fog environment (CoS_FRLM). In: 2020 International Conference on Data Analytics for Business and Industry: Way Towards a Sustainable Economy (ICDABI), During 26–27 October 2020, University of Bahrain, Kingdom of Bahrain. https://doi.org/10.1109/ICDABI 51230.2020.9325619
17. Naik, K.J.: A processing delay tolerant workflow management in cloud-fog computing environment (DTWM_CfS). In: 2020 International Conference on Decision Aid Sciences and Application (DASA 20), During 8th – 9th November 2020, College of Business Administration at the University of Bahrain, Kingdom of Bahrain. https://doi.org/10.1109/DASA51403. 2020.9317201

Author Index

R. Venkataraman et al. (Eds.): ICIoT 2022, CCIS 1727, p. 115, 2023.
https://doi.org/10.1007/978-3-031-28475-5

Printed in the United States
by Baker & Taylor Publisher Services